AN INCIDENT OF TRAVEL

AN INCIDENT OF TRAVEL

*A Record of the People and Places Encountered on a Two
Thousand Mile Motorcar Odyssey Through New York, New
England and Canada, circa 1900*

Arthur Jerome Eddy
Edited by Paul Dennis Sporer

ROLLRIGHT BOOKS

ANZA PUBLISHING, Chester, NY 10918
Rollright Books is an imprint of Anza Publishing
Copyright © 2005 by Anza Publishing

This work is a new, unabridged edition of *Two Thousand Miles on an Automobile, Being a Desultory Narrative of a Trip Through New England, New York, Canada, and the West*, by "Chauffeur", originally published in 1902.

Library of Congress Cataloguing-in-Publication Data
Eddy, Arthur Jerome, 1859–1920.
[Two thousand miles on an automobile]
   An incident of travel / Arthur Jerome Eddy;
   editor Paul D. Sporer.
      p.   cm.
   Originally published as: Two thousand miles on an automobile.
   Philadelphia : J.B. Lippincott, 1902.
   Includes index.
   ISBN 1–932490–26–4 (hardcover: acid-free paper)
   ISBN 1–932490–04–3 (softcover: acid-free paper)
   1. United States — Description and travel.
   2. Eddy, Arthur Jerome, 1859-1920 — Travel — United States.
   3. Automobile travel — United States — History — 20th century.
   4. United States — Social life and customs — 1865-1918.
I. Sporer, Paul D. II. Title.
E168.E21 2004
917.304'911 — dc22   2004015363

Visit AnzaPublishing.com for more information on outstanding authors and titles. Please support our efforts to restore great literature to a place of prominence in our culture.

∞ This book is printed on acid-free paper.

ISBN 1–932490–26–4 (hardcover)
ISBN 1–932490–04–3 (softcover)

Contents

Editor's Preface

Arthur Jerome Eddy (1859-1920), using a very early type of motorcar, made a remarkable journey over country roads through turn-of-the-20th century North America. Writing under the pseudonym "Chauffeur", his travels were presented in a book published in 1902, originally entitled *Two Thousand Miles on an Automobile, Being a Desultory Narrative of a Trip Through New England, New York, Canada, and the West.*

We have restored his work in a new edition, which brings back, in much pleasing tones, a nearly forgotten age when American society was slow, but its people not slow-witted. This is America in transition, a nation only beginning to grasp the great changes that would erupt onto society's stage. Eddy's writing is very informative and entertaining. We feel a sense of sweeping, swirling shades of variety, the melding of different cultures, customs and traditions. Overall, the tone is that of a travelogue, a truthful account of the streets, towns and folk he saw on his journey, but enriched with colorful digressions, some of them satirical, some trenchant. Indeed, Eddy reflects on many issues besides driving, such as philosophy, religion, and politics. Thus, there are fascinating lessons on the mechanics of early automobiles, as well as on local history and community. The "Chauffeur" ties together with remarkable ease disparate elements, and ultimately shows what has been gained and what has been lost in American society.

As the motorcar was so unlike anything that had come before, its presence was always sure to elicit interesting conversation. No doubt everyone recognized Eddy's "machine" as a symbol of the modern age. Some saw it as evidence of positive progress in industry, while others saw it as a revolutionary innovation. Most, however, simply failed to understand the automobile, and it was often perceived to be an impractical and dangerous contraption. Consequently, observers would interpret things in such a way that afforded them safety; for example, Eddy was thought to be a millionaire showing off his latest toy.

Restoration of the work was straightforward. There were relatively few textual errors in the original, and we have preserved all the original spellings, punctuation, and terms. We have also incorporated a new index.

PAUL DENNIS SPORER

CHAPTER 1

Some Preliminary Observations

THE MADDING CROWD

Any woman can drive an electric automobile, any man can drive a steam, but neither man nor woman can drive a gasoline; it follows its own odorous will, and goes or goes not as it feels disposed.

For this very wilfulness the gasoline motor is the most fascinating machine of all. It possesses the subtle attraction of caprice; it constantly offers something to overcome; as in golf, you start out each time to beat your own record. The machine is your tricky and resourceful opponent. When you think it conquered and well-broken to harness, submissive and resigned to your will, behold it is as obstinate as a mule, — balks, kicks, snorts, puffs, blows, or, what is worse, refuses to kick, snort, puff, and blow, but stands in stubborn silence, an obdurate beast which no amount of coaxing, cajoling, cranking will start.

One of the beauties of the beast is its strict impartiality. It shows no more deference to maker than to owner; it moves no more quickly for expert mechanic than for amateur driver. When it balks, it balks, — inventor, manufacturer, mechanic, stand puzzled; suddenly it starts, — they are equally puzzled.

Who has not seen inventors of these capricious motors standing by the roadside scratching their heads in despair, utterly at a loss to know why the stubborn thing does not go? Who has not seen skilled mechanics in blue jeans and unskilled amateurs in jeans of leather, so to speak, flat on their backs under the vehicle, peering upward into the intricacies of the mechanism, trying to find the cause, — the obscure, the hidden source of all their trouble? And then the probing with wires, the tugs with wrenches, the wrestling with screw-drivers, the many trials, — for the most part futile, — the subdued language of the bunkers, and at length, when least expected, a start, and the machine goes off as if nothing at all had been the matter. It is then the skilled driver looks wise and does not betray his surprise to the gaping crowd, just looks as if the start were the anticipated result of his well-directed efforts instead of a chance hit amidst blind gropings.

One cannot but sympathize with the vanity of the French chauffeur who stops his machine in the midst of a crowd when it is working perfectly, makes a few idle passes with wrenches and oil-cans, pulls a lever and is off, all for the pleasure of hearing the populace remark, "He understands his machine. He is a good one." While the poor fellow, who really is in trouble, sweats and groans and all but swears as he works in vain to find what is the matter, to the delight of the onlookers who laugh at what seems to them ignorance and lack of skill.

And why should not these things be? Is not the crowd multitude always with us — or against us? There is no spot so dreary, no country so waste, no highway so far removed from the habitations and haunts of man that a crowd of gaping people will not spring up when an automobile stops for repairs. Choose a plain, the broad expanse of which is unbroken by a sign of man; a wood, the depths of which baffle the eye and tangle the foot; let your automobile stop for so long as sixty seconds, and the populace begin to gather, with the small boy in the van; like birds of prey they perch upon all parts of the machine, choosing by quick intuition those parts most susceptible to injury from weight and contact, until you scarcely can move and do the things you have to do.

The curiosity of the small boy is the forerunner of knowledge, and must be satisfied. It is quite idle to tell him to "Keep away!"; it is worse than useless to lose your temper and order him to "Clear out!"; it is a physical impossibility for him to do either; the law of his being requires him to remain where he is and to indefatigably get in the way. If he did not pry into everything and ask a thousand questions, the thoughtful observer would be fearful lest he were an idiot.

The American small boy is not idiotic; tested by his curiosity concerning automobiles, he is the fruition of the centuries, the genius the world is awaiting, the coming ruler of men and empires, or — who knows? — the coming master of the automobile.

Happily, curiosity is not confined to the small boy; it is but partially suppressed in his elders, — and that is lucky, for his elders, and their horses, can often help.

The young chauffeur is panicky if he comes to a stop on a lonely road, where no human habitation is visible; he fears he may never get away, that no help will come; that he must abandon his machine and walk miles for assistance. The old chauffeur knows better. It matters not to him how lonely the road, how remote the spot, one or two plaintive blasts of the horn and, like mushrooms, human beings begin to spring up; whence they come is a mystery to you; why they come equally a mystery to them, but come they will, and to help they are willing, to the harnessing of horses and the dragging of the heavy machine to such place as you desire.

This willingness, not to say eagerness. on the part of the farmer, the truckman, the liveryman, in short, the owner of horses, to help out a machine he despises, which frightens his horses and causes him no end of trouble, is an interesting trait of human nature; a veritable heaping of coals of fire. So long as the machine is careering along in the full tide of glory, clearing and monopolizing the highway, the horse owner wishes it in Hades; but let the machine get into trouble, and the same horse owner will pull up out of the ditch into which he has been driven, hitch his horses to the cause of his scare, haul it to his stable, and make room by turning his Sunday carryall into the lane, and four farmers, three truckmen, and two liverymen out of five will refuse all offers of payment for their trouble.

But how galling to the pride of the automobilist to see a pair of horses patiently pulling his machine along the highway, and how he fights against such an unnatural ending of a day's run.

The real chauffeur, the man who knows his machine, who can run it, who is something more than a puller of levers and a twister of wheels, will not seek or permit the aid of horse or any other power, except where the trouble is such that no human ingenuity can repair on the road.

It is seldom the difficulty is such that repairs cannot be made on the spot. The novice looks on in despair, the experienced driver considers a moment, makes use of the tools and few things he has with him, and goes on.

It is astonishing how much can be done with few tools and practically no supplies. A packing blows out; if you have no asbestos, brown paper, or even newspaper saturated with oil, will do for the time being; if a wheel has to be taken off, a fence-rail makes an excellent jack; if a chain is to be riveted, an axe or even a stone makes a good dolly-bar and your wrench an excellent riveting hammer; if screws, or nuts, or bolts drop off, — and they do, — and you have no extra, a glance at the machine is sure to disclose duplicates that can be removed temporarily to the more essential places.

Then, too, no one has ever exhausted the limitless resources of a farmer's wagon-shed. In it you find the accumulations of generations, bits of every conceivable thing, — all rusty, of course, and seemingly worthless, but sure to serve your purpose on a pinch, and so accessible, never locked; just go in and help yourself. Nowadays farmers use and abuse so much complicated machinery, that it is more than likely one could construct entire an automobile from the odds and ends of a half-dozen farm-yards.

All boys and most girls — under twelve — say, "Gimme a ride;" some boys and a few girls — over twelve — say, "You look lonesome, mister." What the hoodlums of the cities say will hardly bear repetition. In spite of its swiftness the automobile offers opportunities for studying human nature appreciated only by the driver.

The city hoodlum is a most aggressive individual; he is not invariably in tattered clothes, and is by no means confined to the alleys and side streets. The hoodlum element is a constituent part of human nature, present in everyone; the classification of the individual depending simply upon the depth at which the turbulent element is buried, upon the number and thickness of the overlying strata of civilization and refinement. In the recognized hoodlum the obnoxious element is quite at the surface; in the best of us it is only too apt to break forth, — no man can be considered an absolutely extinct volcano.

One can readily understand why owners and drivers of horses should feel and even exhibit a marked aversion towards the automobile, since, from their stand-point, it is an unmitigated nuisance; but why the hoodlums who stand about the street corners should be animated by a seemingly irresistible desire to hurl stones and brickbats — as well as epithets — at passing automobiles is a mystery worth solving; it presents an interesting problem in psychology. What is the mental process occasioned by the sudden appearance of an automobile, and which results in the hurling of the first missile which comes to hand? It must be a reversion to savage instincts, the instinct of the chase; something strange comes quickly into view; it makes a strange noise, emits, perhaps, a strange odor, is passing quickly and about to escape; it must be killed, hence the brickbat. Uncontrollable impulse! poor hoodlum, he cannot help it; if he could restrain the hand and stay the brickbat he would not be a hoodlum, but a man. Time and custom have tamed him so that he lets horses, bicycles, and carriages pass; he can't quite help slinging a stone at an advertising van or any strange vehicle, while the automobile is altogether too much.

That it is the machine which rouses his savage instincts is clear from the fact that rarely is anything thrown at the occupants. Complete satisfaction is found in hitting the thing itself; no doubt regret would be felt if anyone were injured, but if the stone resounds upon the iron frame of the moving devil, the satisfaction is felt that the best of us might experience from hitting the scaly sides of a slumbering sea-monster, for hit him we would, though at immediate risk of perdition.

The American hoodlum has, withal, his good points. If you are not in trouble, he will revile and stone you; if in trouble, he will commiserate and assist. He is quick to put his shoulder to the wheel and push, pull or lift; often with mechanical insight superior to the unfortunate driver he will discern the difficulty and suggest the remedy; dirt has no terrors for him, oil is his delight, grease the goal of his desires; mind you, all this concerns the American hoodlum or the hoodlum of indefinite or of Irish extraction; it applies not to the Teutonic or other hoodlum. He will pass you by with phlegmatic indifference, he will not throw things at you, neither will he help you unless strongly appealed to, and then not over-zealously or over-intelligently; his application is short-lived and he hurries on; but the other hoodlum will stay with you all night if necessary, finding, no doubt, the automobile a pleasant diversion from a bed on the grass.

But the dissension a quarter will cause! A battle royal was once produced by a dollar. They had all assisted, but, like the workers in the vineyard, some had come early and some late. The automobile, in trying to turn on a narrow road, had dropped off the side into low wet ground; the early comers could not quite get it back, but with the aid of the later it was done; the division of a dollar left behind raised the old, old problem. Unhappily, it fell into the hands of a late comer for distribution, and it was his contention that the final lift did the work, that all previous effort was so much wasted energy; the early comers contended that the reward should be in proportion to expenditure of time and muscle and not measured by actual achievement, — a discussion not without force on both sides, but cut short by a scrimmage involving far more force than the discussion. All of which goes to show the disturbing influence of money, for in all truth those who had assisted did not expect any reward; they first laughed to see the machine in the ditch, and then turned to like tigers to get it out.

This whole question of paying for services in connection with automobiling is as interesting as it is new. The people are not adjusted to the strange vehicle. A man with a white elephant could probably travel from New York to San Francisco without disbursing a penny for the keeping of his animal. Farmers and even liverymen would keep and feed it on the way without charge. It is a good deal so with an automobile; it is still sufficiently a curiosity to command respect and attention. The farmer is glad to have it stop in front of his door or put up in his shed; he will supply it with oil and water. The blacksmith would rather have it stop at his shop for repair than at his rival's, — it gives him a little notoriety, something to talk about. So it is with the liveryman at night; he is, as a rule, only too glad to have the novelty under his roof, and takes pride in showing it to the visiting townsfolk. They do not know what to charge, and therefore charge nothing. It is often with difficulty anything can be forced upon them; they are quite averse to accepting gratuities; meanwhile, the farmer, whose horse and cart have taken up far less room and caused far less trouble, pays the fixed charge.

These conditions prevail only in localities where automobiles are seen infrequently. Along the highways where they travel frequently all is quite changed; many a stable will not house them at any price, and those that will, charge goodly sums for the service.

It is one thing to own an automobile, another thing to operate it. It is one thing to sit imposingly at the steering-wheel until something goes wrong, and quite another thing to repair and go on.

There are chauffeurs and chauffeurs, — the latter wear the paraphernalia and are photographed, while the former are working under the machines. You can tell the difference by the goggles. The sham chauffeur sits in front and turns the wheel, the real one sits behind and takes things as they come; the former wears the goggles, the latter finds sufficient protection in the smut on the end of his nose.

There is every excuse for relying helplessly on an expert mechanic if you have no mechanical ingenuity, or are averse to getting dirty and grimy; but that is not automobiling; it is being run about in a huge perambulator.

The real chauffeur knows every moment by the sound and "feel" of his machine exactly what it is doing, the amount of gasoline it is taking, whether the lubrication is perfect, the character and heat of the spark, the condition of almost every screw, nut, and bolt, and he runs his machine accordingly; at the first indication of anything wrong he stops and takes the stitch in time that saves ninety and nine later. The sham chauffeur sits at the wheel, and in the security of ignorance runs gayly along until his machine is a wreck; he may have hours, days, or even weeks of blind enjoyment, but the end is inevitable, and the repairs costly; then he blames everyone but himself,—blames the maker for not making a machine that may be operated by inexperience forever, blames the men in his stable for what reason he knows not, blames the roads, the country, everything and everybody—but himself.

It is amusing to hear the sham chauffeur talk. When things go well, he does it; when they go wrong, it is the fault of someone else; if he makes a successful run, the mechanic with him is a nonentity; if he breaks down, the mechanic is his only resource. It is more interesting to hear the mechanic—the real chauffeur—talk when he is flat on his back making good the mistakes of his master, but his conversation could not be printed *verbatim et literatim,*—it is explosive and without a muffler.

The man who cannot run his machine a thousand miles without expert assistance should make no pretense to being a chauffeur, for he is not one. The chauffeur may use mechanics whenever he can find them; but if he can't find them, he gets along just as well; and when he does use them it is not for information and advice, but to do just the things he wants done and no more. The skilled enthusiast would not think of letting even an expert from the factory do anything to his machine, unless he stood over him and watched every movement; as soon would a lover of horses permit his hostlers to dope his favorite mount.

CHAPTER 2

The Machine Used

MAKING READY TO START

The machine was just an ordinary twelve hundred dollar single-cylinder American machine, with neither improvements nor attachments to especially strengthen it for a long tour; and it had seen constant service since January without any return to the shop for repairs.

It was rated eight and one-half horsepower; but, as everyone knows, American machines are overrated as a rule, while foreign machines are greatly underrated. A twelve horsepower American machine may mean not more than eight or ten; a twelve horsepower French machine, with its four cylinders, means not less than sixteen.

The foreign manufacturer appreciates the advantage of having it said that his eight horsepower machine will run faster and climb better than the eight horsepower machine of a rival maker; hence the tendency to increase the power without changing the nominal rating. The American manufacturer caters to the demand for machines of high power by advancing the nominal rating quite beyond the power actually developed.

But already things are changing here, and makers show a disposition to rate their machines low, for the sake of astonishing in performance. A man dislikes to admit his machine is rated at forty horsepower and to acknowledge defeat by a machine rated at twenty, when the truth is that each machine is probably about thirty.

The tendency at the present moment is decidedly towards the French type, — two or four cylinders placed in front.

In the construction of racing-cars and high-speed machines for such roads as they have on the other side, we have much to learn from the French, — and we have been slow in learning it. The conceit of the American mechanic amounts often to blind stubbornness, but the ease with which the foreign machines have passed the American in all races on smooth roads has opened the eyes of our builders; the danger just now is that they will go to the other extreme and copy too blindly.

In the hands of experts, the foreign racing-cars are the most perfect road locomotives yet devised; for touring over American roads in the hands of the amateur they are worse than useless; and even experts have great difficulty in running week in and week out without serious breaks and delays. To use a slang phrase, "They will not stand the racket." However "stunning" they look on asphalt and macadam with their low, rakish bodies, resplendent in red and polished brass, on country roads they are very frequently failures. A thirty horsepower foreign machine costing ten or twelve thousand dollars, accompanied by one or more expert mechanics, may make a brilliant showing for a week or so; but when the time is up, the ordinary, cheap, country-looking, American automobile will be found a close second at the finish; not that it is a finer piece of machinery, for it is not; but it has been developed under the adverse conditions prevailing in this country and is built to surmount them. The maker in this country who runs his machine one hundred miles from his factory, would find fewer difficulties between Paris and Berlin.

The temptation is great to purchase a foreign machine on sight; resist the temptation until you have ridden in it over a hundred miles of sandy, clayey, and hilly American roads; you may then defer the purchase indefinitely, unless you expect to carry along a man.

Machine for machine, regardless of price, the comparison is debatable; but price for price, there is no comparison whatsoever; in fact, there is no inexpensive imported machine which compares for a moment with the American product.

A single-cylinder motor possesses a few great advantages to compensate for many disadvantages; it has fewer parts to get out of order, and troubles can be much more quickly located and overcome. Two, three, and four cylinders run with less vibration and are better in every way, except that with every cylinder added the chances of troubles are multiplied, and the difficulty of locating them increased. Each cylinder must have its own lubrication, its ignition, intake, and exhaust mechanisms, — the quartette that is responsible for nine-tenths of the stops.

Beyond eight or ten horsepower the single cylinder is hardly practicable. The kick from the explosion is too violent, the vibration and strain too great, and power is lost in transmission. But up to eight or ten horsepower the single-cylinder motor with a heavy fly-wheel is practicable, runs very smoothly at high speeds, mounts hills and ploughs mud quite successfully. The American ten horsepower single-cylinder motor will go faster and farther on our roads than most foreign double-cylinder machines of the same horsepower. It will last longer and require less repairs.

The amateur who is not a pretty good mechanic and who wishes to tour without the assistance of an expert will do well to use the single-cylinder motor; he will have trouble enough with that without seeking further complications by the adoption of multiple cylinders.

It is quite practicable to attain speeds of from twenty to thirty miles per hour with a single-cylinder motor, but for bad roads and hilly countries a low gear with a maximum of twenty to twenty-five miles per hour is better. The average for the day will be higher because better speed is maintained through heavy roads and on up grades.

So far as resiliency is concerned, there is no comparison between the French double-tube tire and the heavy American single tube, — the former is far ahead, and is, of course, easily repaired on the road, but it does not seem to stand the severe wear of American roads, and it is very easily punctured. Our highways both in and out of cities are filled with things that cut, and bristle with wire-nails. The heavy American single-tube tire holds out quite well; it gets many deep cuts and takes nails like a pin-cushion, but comparatively few go through. The weight of the tire makes it rather hard riding, very hard, indeed, as compared with a fine Michelin.

There are many devices for carrying luggage, but for getting a good deal into a small compass there is nothing equal to a big Scotch hold-all. It is waterproof to begin with, and holds more than a small steamer-trunk. It can be strapped in or under the machine anywhere. Trunks and hat-boxes may remain with the express companies, always within a few hours' call.

What to wear is something of a problem. In late autumn and winter fur is absolutely essential to comfort. Even at fifteen or twenty miles an hour the wind is penetrating and goes through everything but the closest of fur. For women, fur or leather-lined coats are comfortable even when the weather seems still quite warm.

Leather coats are a great protection against both cold and dust. Unhappily, most people who have no machines of their own, when invited to ride, have nothing fit to wear; they dress too thinly, wear hats that blow off, and they altogether are, and look, quite unhappy — to the great discomfort of those with them. It is not a bad plan to have available one or two good warm coats for the benefit of guests, and always carry waterproof coats and lap-covers. In emergency, thin black oil-cloth, purchasable at any country store, makes a good water-proof covering.

Whoever is running a machine must be prepared for emergencies, for at any moment it may be necessary to get underneath.

The man who is going to master his own machine must expect to get dirty; dust, oil, and grime plentifully distributed, — but dirt is picturesque, even if objectionable. Character is expressed in dirt; the bright and shining school-boy face is devoid of interest, an artificial product, quite unnatural; the smutty street urchin is an actor on life's stage, every daub, spot, and line an essential part of his make-up.

The spic and span may go well with a coach and four, but not with the automobile. Imagine an engineer driving his locomotive in blue coat, yellow waistcoat, and ruffles, — quite as appropriate as a fastidious dress on the automobile.

People are not yet quite accustomed to the grime of automobiling; they tolerate the dust of the golf links, the dirt of base-ball and cricket, the mud of foot-ball, and would ridicule the man who failed to dress appropriately for those games, but the mechanic's blouse or leather coat of automobiling, the gloves saturated with oil — these are comparatively unfamiliar sights; hence men are seen starting off for a hard run in ducks and serges, sacks, cutaways, even frocks, and hats of all styles; give a farmer a silk hat and patent leather boots to wear while threshing, and he would match them.

Every sport has its own appropriate costume, and the costume is not the result of arbitrary choice, but of natural selection; if we hunt, fish, or play any outdoor game, sooner or later we find ourselves dressing like our associates. The tenderfoot may put on his cowboy's suit a little too soon and look and be very uncomfortable, but the costume is essential to success in the long run.

The Russian cap so commonly seen is an affectation, — it catches the wind and is far from comfortable. The best head covering is a closely fitting Scotch cap.

CHAPTER 3

The Start

"IS THIS ROAD TO —"

The trip was not premeditated — it was not of malice aforethought; it was the outcome of an idle suggestion made one hot summer afternoon, and decided upon in the moment. Within the same half-hour a telegram was sent the Professor inviting him for a ride to Buffalo. Beyond that point there was no thought, — merely a nebulous notion that might take form if everything went well.

Hampered by no announcements, with no record to make or break, the trip was for pleasure, — a mid-summer jaunt. We did intend to make the run to Buffalo as fast as roads would permit, — but for exhilaration only, and not with any thought of making a record that would stand against record-making machines, driven by record-breaking men.

It is much better to start for nowhere and get there than to start for somewhere and fall by the wayside. Just keep going, and the machine will carry you beyond your expectations.

The Professor knew nothing about machinery and less about an automobile, but where ignorance is bliss it is double-distilled folly to know anything about the eccentricities of an automobile.

To enjoy automobiling, one must know either all or nothing about the machine, — a little knowledge is a dangerous thing; on the part of the guest it leads to all sorts of apprehensions, on the part of the chauffeur to all sorts of experiments. About five hundred miles is the limit of a man's ignorance; he then knows enough to make trouble; at the end of another five hundred he is of assistance, at the end of the third he will run the machine himself — your greatest pleasure is in the first five hundred. With some precocious individuals these figures may be reduced somewhat.

The Professor adjusted his spectacles and looked at the machine:

"A very wonderful contrivance, and one that requires some skill to operate. From lack of experience, I cannot hope to be of much practical assistance at first, but possibly a theoretical knowledge of the laws and principles governing things mechanical may be of service in an emergency. Since receiving your telegram, I have brushed up a little my knowledge of both kinematics and dynamics, though it is quite apparent that the operation of these machines, accompanied, as it is said, by many restraints and perturbations, falls under the latter branch. In view of the possibility — remote, I trust — of the machine refusing to go, I have devoted a little time to statics, and therefore feel that I shall be something more than a supercargo."

"Well, you *are* equipped, Professor; no doubt your knowledge will prove useful."

"Knowledge is always useful if people in this busy age would only pause to make use of it. Mechanics has been defined as the application of pure mathematics to produce or modify motion in inferior bodies; what could be more apt? Is it not our intention to produce or modify motion in this inferior body before us?"

Days after the Professor found the crank a more useful implement for the inducing of motion.

It was Thursday morning, August 1, at exactly seven o'clock, that we passed south on Michigan Avenue towards South Chicago and Hammond. A glorious morning, neither hot nor cold, but just deliciously cool, with some promise — afterwards more than fulfilled — of a warm day.

The hour was early, policemen few, streets clear, hence fast speed could be made.

As we passed Zion Temple, near Twelfth Street, the home of the Dowieites, the Professor said:

"A very remarkable man, that Dowie."

"A fraud and an impostor," I retorted, reflecting current opinion.

"Possibly; but we all impose more or less upon one another; he has simply made a business of his imposition. Did you ever meet him?"

"No; it's hardly worthwhile."

"It is worth while to meet any man who influences or controls a considerable body of his fellow-men. The difference between Mohammed and Joseph Smith is of degree rather than kind. Dowie is down towards the small end of the scale, but he is none the less there, and differs in kind from your average citizen in his power to influence and control others. I crossed the lake with him one night and spent the evening in conversation."

"What are your impressions of the man?"

"A shrewd, hard-headed, dogmatic Scotchman, — who neither smokes nor drinks."

"Who calls himself Elijah come to earth again."

"I had the temerity to ask him concerning his pretensions in that direction, and he said, substantially, 'I make no claims or assertions, but the Bible says Elijah will return to earth; it does not say in what form or how he will manifest himself; he might choose your personality; he might choose mine; he has not chosen yours, there are some evidences that he has chosen mine.'"

"Proof most conclusive."

"It satisfies his followers. After all, perhaps it does not matter so much what we believe as how we believe."

A few moments later we were passing the new Christian Science Temple on Drexel Boulevard, — a building quite simple and delightful, barring some garish lamps in front.

"There is another latter-day sect," said the Professor; "one of the phenomena of the nineteenth century."

"You would not class them with the Dowieites?"

"By no means, but an interesting part of a large whole which embraces at one extreme the Dowieites. The connecting link is faith. But the very architecture of the temple we have just passed illustrates the vast interval that separates the two."

"Then you judge a sect by its buildings?"

"Every faith has its own architecture. The temple at Karnak and the tabernacle at Salt Lake City are petrifactions of faith. In time the places of worship are the only tangible remains — witness Stonehenge."

Chicago boasts the things she has not and slights the things she has; she talks of everything but the lake and her broad and almost endless boulevards, yet these are her chief glories.

For miles and miles and miles one can travel boulevards upon which no traffic teams are allowed. From Fort Sheridan, twenty-five miles north, to far below Jackson Park to the south there is an unbroken stretch. Some day Sheridan Road will extend to Milwaukee, ninety miles from Chicago.

One may reach Jackson Park, the old World's Fair site, by three fine boulevards, — Michigan, broad and straight; Drexel, with its double driveways and banks of flowers, trees, and shrubbery between; Grand, with its three driveways, and so wide one cannot recognize an acquaintance on the far side, cannot even see the policeman frantically motioning to slow down.

It does not matter which route is taken to the Park, the good roads end there. We missed our way, and went eighteen miles to Hammond, over miles of poor pavement and unfinished roads. That was a pull which tried nerves and temper, — to find at the end there was another route which involved but a short distance of poor going. It is all being improved, and soon there will be a good road to Hammond.

Through Indiana from Hammond to Hobart the road is macadamized and in perfect condition; we reached Hobart at half-past nine; no stop was made. At Crocker two pails of water were added to the cooling tank.

At Porter the road was lost for a second time, — exasperating. At Chesterton four gallons of gasoline were taken and a quick run made to Burdick.

The roads are now not so good, — not bad, but just good country roads, some stretches of gravel, but generally clay, with some sand here and there. The country is rolling, but no steep hills.

Up to this time the machine had required no attention, but just beyond Otis, while stopping to inquire the way, we discovered a rusty round nail embedded to the head in the right rear tire. The tire showed no signs of deflation, but on drawing the nail the air followed, showing a puncture. As the nail was scarcely three-quarters of an inch long, — not long enough to go clear through and injure the inner coating on the opposite side, — it was entirely practical to reinsert and run until it worked out. A very fair temporary repair might have been made by first dipping the nail in a tire cement, but the nail was rusty and stuck very well.

An hour later, at La Porte, the nail was still doing good service and no leak could be detected. We wired back to Chicago to have an extra tire sent on ahead.

From Chicago to La Porte, by way of Hobart, the roads are excellent, excepting always the few miles near South Chicago. Keep to the south — even as far south as Valparaiso — rather than to the north, near the lake. The roads are hilly and sandy near the lake.

Beware the so-called road map; it is a snare and a delusion. A road which seems most seductive on the bicycler's road map may be a sea of sand or a veritable quagmire, but with a fine bicycle path at the side. As you get farther east these cinder paths are protected by law, with heavy fines for driving thereon; it requires no little restraint to plough miles and miles through bottomless mud on a narrow road in the Mohawk valley with a superb three-foot cinder path against your very wheels. The machine of its own accord will climb up now and then; it requires all the vigilance of a law-abiding driver to keep it in the mud, where it is so unwilling to travel.

So far as finding and keeping the road is concerned, — and it is a matter of great concern in this vast country, where roads, cross-roads, forks, and all sorts of snares and delusions abound without sign-boards to point the way, — the following directions may be given once for all:

If the proposed route is covered by any automobile hand-book or any automobile publication, get it, carry it with you and be guided by it; all advice of ancient inhabitants to the contrary notwithstanding.

If there is no publication covering the route, take pains to get from local automobile sources information about the several possible routes to the principal towns which you wish to make.

If you can get no information at all from automobile sources, you can make use — with great caution — of bicycle road maps, of the maps rather than the redlined routes.

About the safest course is to spread out the map and run a straight line between the principal points on the proposed route, note the larger villages, towns, and cities near the line so drawn, make a list of them in the order they come from the starting-point, and simply inquire at each of these points for the best road to the next.

If the list includes places of fair size, — say, from one to ten or twenty thousand inhabitants, it is reasonably certain that the roads connecting such places will be about as good as there are in the vicinity; now and then a better road may be missed, but, in the long run, that does not matter much, and the advantage of keeping quite close to the straight line tells in the way of mileage.

It is usually worse than useless to inquire in any place about the roads beyond a radius of fifteen or twenty miles; plenty of answers to all questions will be forthcoming, but they simply mislead. In these days of railroads, farmers no longer make long overland drives.

It is much easier to get information in small villages than in cities. In a city about all one can learn is how to get out by the shortest cut. Once out, the first farmer will give information about the roads beyond.

In wet weather the last question will be, "Is the road clayey or bottomless anywhere?"

In dry weather, "Is there any deep, soft sand, and are there any sand hills?"

The judgment of a man who is looking at the machine while he is giving information is biased by the impressions as to what the machine can do; make allowances for this and get, if possible, an accurate description of the condition of any road which is pronounced impassable, for you alone know what the machine can do and many a road others think you cannot cover is made with ease

To the farmer the automobile is a traction engine, and he advises the route accordingly; he will even speculate whether a given bridge will support the extraordinary load.

Once we were directed to go miles out of our way over a series of hills to avoid a stretch of road freshly covered with broken stone, because our solicitous friends were sure the stones would cut the rubber tires.

On the other hand, in Michigan, a well meaning old lady sent us straight against the very worst of sand hills, not a weed, stone, or hard spot on it, so like quicksand that the wheels sank as they revolved; it was the only hill from which we retreated, to find that farmers avoided that particular road on account of that notorious hill, to find also a good, well-travelled road one mile farther around. These instances are mentioned here to show how hazardous it is to accept blindly directions given.

"Is this the road to—?" is the chauffeur's ever recurring shout to people as he whizzes by. Four times out of five he gets a blank stare or an idiotic smile. Now and then he receives a quick "Yes" or "No."

If time permits to stop and discuss the matter at length, do so with a man; if passing quickly, ask a woman.

A woman will reply before a man comprehends what is asked; the feminine mind is so much more alert than the masculine; then, too, a woman would rather know what a man is saying than watch a machine, while a man would rather see the machine than listen; — in many ways the automobile differentiates the sexes.

Of a group of school children, the girls will answer more quickly and accurately than the boys. What they know, they seem to know positively. A boy's wits go wool gathering; he is watching the wheels go round.

At Carlyle, on the way to South Bend, the tire was leaking slightly, the nail had worked out. The road is a fine wide macadam, somewhat rolling as South Bend is approached.

By the road taken South Bend is about one hundred miles from

Chicago, — the distance actually covered was some six or eight miles farther, on account of wanderings from the straight and narrow path. The hour was exactly two fifty-three, nearly eight hours out, an average of about twelve and one-half miles an hour, including all stops, and stops count in automobiling; they pull the average down by jumps.

The extra tire was to be at Elkhart, farther on, and the problem was to make the old one hold until that point would be reached. Just as we were about to insert a plug to take the place of the nail, a bicycle repairer suggested rubber bands. A dozen small bands were passed through the little fork made by the broken eye of a large darning-needle, stretched tight over a wooden handle into which the needle had been inserted; some tire cement was injected into the puncture, and the needle carrying the stretched bands deftly thrust clear through; on withdrawing the needle the bands remained, plugging the hole so effectually that it showed no leak until some weeks later, when near Boston, the air began to work slowly through the fabric.

Heavy and clumsy as are the large single-tube tires, it is quite practicable to carry an extra one, though we did not. One is pretty sure to have punctures, — though two in twenty-six hundred miles are not many.

Nearly an hour was spent at South Bend; the river road, following the trolley line, was taken to Elkhart.

Near Osceola a bridge was down for repairs; the stream was quite wide and swift but not very deep. From the broken bridge the bottom seemed to be sand and gravel, and the approaches on each side were not too steep. There was nothing to do but go through or lose many miles in going round. Putting on all power we went through with no difficulty whatsoever, the water at the deepest being about eighteen to twenty inches, somewhat over the hubs. If the bottom of the little stream had been soft and sticky, or filled with boulders, fording would have been out of the question. Before attempting a stream, one must make sure of the bottom; the depth is of less importance.

We did not run into Elkhart, but passed about two miles south in sight of the town, arriving at Goshen at four fifteen. The roads all through here seem to be excellent. From Goshen our route was through Benton and Ligonier, arriving at Kendallville at exactly eight o'clock.

The Professor with painstaking accuracy kept a log of the run, noting every stop and the time lost.

In this first day's run of thirteen hours, the distance covered by route taken was one hundred and seventy miles; deducting all stops, the actual running time was nine hours and twenty minutes, an average of eighteen miles per hour while the machine was in motion.

For an ordinary road machine this is a high average over so long a stretch, but the weather was perfect and the machine working like a clock. The roads were very good on the whole, and, while the country was rolling, the grades were not so steep as to compel the use of the slow gear to any great extent.

The machine was geared rather high for any but favorable conditions, and could make thirty-five miles an hour on level macadam, and race down grade at an even higher rate. Before reaching Buffalo we found the gearing too high for some grades and for deep sand.

On the whole, the roads of Northern Indiana are good, better than the roads of any adjoining State, and we were told the roads of the entire State are very good. The system of improvement under State laws seems to be quite advanced. It is a little galling to the people of Illinois, Michigan, and Ohio to find the humble Hoosier is far ahead in the matter of road building. If all the roads between Chicago and New York averaged as good as those of Indiana, the trip would present fewer difficulties and many more delights.

The Professor notes that up to this point nine and three-quarters gallons of gasoline have been consumed, — seventeen miles to the gallon. When a motor is working perfectly, the consumption of gasoline is always a pretty fair indication of the character of the roads. Our machine was supposed to make twenty miles to the gallon, and so it would on level roads, with the spark well advance and the intake valve operating to a nicety; but under adverse conditions more gasoline is used, and with the hill-climbing gear four times the gasoline is used per mile.

The long run of this first day was most encouraging; but the test is not the first day, nor the second, nor even the first week, nor the second, but the steady pull of week in and week out. With every mile there is a theoretical decrease in the life and total efficiency of the machine; after a run of five hundred or a thousand miles this decrease is very perceptible. The trouble is that while the distance covered increases in arithmetical progression, the deterioration of the machine is in geometrical. During the first few days a good machine requires comparatively little attention each day; during the last weeks of a long tour it requires double the attention and ten times the work.

No one who has not tried it can appreciate the great strain and the wear and tear incidental to long rides on American roads. Going at twenty or twenty-five miles an hour in a machine with thirty-two-inch wheels and short wheel-base gives about the same exercise one gets on a horse; one is lifted from the seat and thrown from side to side, until you learn to ride the machine as you would a trotter and take the bumps, accordingly. It is trying to the nerves and the temper, it exercises every muscle in the body, and at night one is ready for a good rest.

Lovers of the horse frequently say that automobiling is to coaching as steam yachting is to sailing, — all of which argues the densest ignorance concerning automobiling, since there is no sport which affords anything like the same measure of exhilaration and danger, and requires anything like the same amount of nerve, dash, and daring. Since the days of Roman chariot racing the records of man describe nothing that parallels automobile racing, and, so far as we have any knowledge, chariot racing, save for the plaudits of vast throngs of spectators, was tame and uneventful compared with the frightful pace of sixty and eighty miles an hour in a throbbing, bounding, careering road locomotive, over roads practically unknown, passing persons, teams, vehicles, cattle, obstacles, and obstructions of all kinds, with a thousand hair-breadth escapes from wreck and destruction.

The sport may not be pretty and graceful; it lacks the sanction of convention, the halo of tradition. It does not admit of smart gowns and gay trappings; it is the last product of a mechanical age, the triumph of mechanical ingenuity, the harnessing of mechanical forces for pleasure instead of profit, — the automobile is the mechanical horse, and, while not as graceful, is infinitely more powerful, capricious, and dangerous than the ancient beast.

CHAPTER 4

Into Ohio

THE RAILROAD SPIKE

A five o'clock call, though quite in accordance with orders, was received with some resentment and responded to reluctantly, the Professor remarking that it seemed but fair to give the slow-going sun a reasonable start as against the automobile.

About fifty minutes were given to a thorough examination of the machine. Beyond the tightening of perhaps six or eight nuts there was nothing to do, everything was in good shape. But there is hardly a screw or nut on a new automobile that will not require tightening after a little hard usage; this is quite in the nature of things, and not a fault. It is only under work that every part of the machine settles into place. It is of vital importance during the first few days of a long tour to go over every screw, nut, and bolt, however firm and tight they may appear.

In time many of the screws and nuts will rust and corrode in place so as to require no more attention, but all that are subjected to great vibration will work loose, soon or late. The addition of one or two extra nuts, if there is room, helps somewhat; but where it is practical, rivet or upset the bolt with a few blows of the hammer, or with a punch, cold chisel, or even screw-driver jam the threads near the nut, — these destructive measures to be adopted only at points where it is rarely necessary to remove the bolts, and where possibilities of trouble from loosening are greater than any trouble that may be caused by destroying the threads.

We left Kendallville at ten minutes past seven; a light rain was falling which laid the dust for the first two miles. With top, side curtains, and boot we were perfectly dry, but the air was uncomfortably cool.

At Butler, an hour and a half later, the rain was coming down hard, and the roads were beginning to be slippery, with about two inches of mud and water.

We caught up with an old top buggy, curtains all on and down, a crate of ducks behind, the horse slowly jogging along at about three miles per hour. We wished to pass, but at each squawk of the horn the old lady inside simply put her hand through under the rear curtain and felt to see what was the matter with her ducks. We were obliged to shout to attract her attention.

In the country the horn is not so good for attracting attention as a loud gong. The horn is mistaken for dinner-horns and distant sounds of farm-yard life. One may travel for some distance behind a wagon-load of peo-ple, trying to attract their attention with blasts on the horn, and see them casually look from side to side to see whence the sound proceeds, appar-ently without suspecting it could come from the highway.

The gong, however, is a well-known means of warning, used by police and fire departments and by trolley lines, and it works well in the country.

For some miles the Professor had been drawing things about him, and as he buttoned a newspaper under his coat remarked, "The modern news-paper is admirably designed to keep people warm—both inside and out. Under circumstances such as these one can understand why it is some-times referred to as a 'blanket sheet.' The morning is almost cold enough for a 'yellow journal,'" and the Professor wandered on into an abstract dissertation upon journalism generally, winding up with the remark that, "It was the support of the yellow press which defeated Bryan;" but then the Professor is neither a politician nor the son of a politician—being a Scotchman, and therefore a philosopher and dogmatist. The pessimistic vein in his remarks was checked by the purchase of a reversible waterproof shooting-jacket at Butler, several sizes too large, but warm; and the Profes-sor remarked, as he gathered its folds about him, "I was never much of a shot, but with this I think I'll make a hit."

"Strange how the thickness of a garment alters our views of things in general," I remarked.

"My dear fellow, philosophy is primarily a matter of food; secondarily, a matter of clothes: it does not concern the head at all."

At Butler we tightened the clutches, as the roads were becoming heavier.

At Edgerton the skies were clearing, the roads were so much better that the last three miles into Ridgeville were made in ten minutes.

At Napoleon someone advised the road through Bowling Green instead of what is known as the River road; in a moment of aberration we took the advice. For some miles the road was being repaired and almost im-passable; farther on it seemed to be a succession of low, yellow sand-hills, which could only be surmounted by getting out, giving the machine all its power, and adding our own in the worst places.

Sand — deep, bottomless sand — is the one obstacle an automobile cannot overcome. It is possible to traverse roads so rough that the machine is well-nigh wrenched apart; to ride over timbers, stones, and boulders; plough through mud; but sand — deep, yielding sand — brings one to a stand-still. A reserve force of twenty or thirty horsepower will get through most places, but in dry weather every chauffeur dreads hearing the word sand, and anxiously inquires concerning the character of the sandy places.

Happily, when the people say the road is "sandy," they usually mean two or three inches of light soil, or gravelly sand over a firm foundation of some kind — that is all right; if there is a firm bottom, it does not matter much how deep the dust on top; the machine will go at nearly full speed over two or three inches of soft stuff; but if on cross-examination it is found that by sand they mean sand, and that ahead is a succession of sand ridges that are sand from base to summit. with no path, grass, or weeds upon which a wheel can find footing, then inquire for some way around and take it; it might be possible to plough through, but that is demoralizing on a hot day.

Happily, along most sandy roads and up most hills of sand there are firm spots along one side or the other, patches of weeds or grass which afford wheel-hold. Usually the surface of the sand is slightly firmer and the large automobile tires ride on it fairly well. As a rule, the softest, deepest, and most treacherous places in sand are the tracks where wagons travel — these are like quicksand.

The sun was hot, the sand was deep, and we had pushed and tugged until the silence was ominous; at length the lowering clouds of wrath broke, and the Professor said things that cannot be repeated.

By way of apology, he said, afterwards, while shaking the sand out of his shoes, "It is difficult to preserve the serenity of the classroom under conditions so very dissimilar. I understand now why the golf-playing parson swears in a bunker. It is not right. but it is very human. It is the recrudescence of the old Adam, the response of humanity to emergency. Education and religion prepare us for the commonplace; nature takes care of the extraordinary. The Quaker hits back before he thinks. It is so much easier to repent than prevent. On the score of scarcity alone, an ounce of prevention is worth several tons of repentance; and — "

It was so apparent that the Professor was losing himself in abstractions, that I quietly let the clutches slip until the machine came to a stop, when the Professor looked anxiously down and said, —

"Is the blamed thing stuck again?"

We turned off the Bowling Green road to the River road, which is not only better, but more direct from Napoleon to Perrysburg. It was the road we originally intended to take; it was down on our itinerary, and in automobiling it is better to stick to first intentions.

The road follows the bank of the river up hill and down, through ravines and over creeks; it is hard, hilly, and picturesque; high speed was quite out of the question.

Not far from Three Rivers we came to a horse tethered among the trees by the road-side; of course, on hearing and seeing the automobile and while we were yet some distance away, it broke its tether and was off on a run up the road, which meant that unless someone intervened it would fly on ahead for miles. Happily, in this instance some men caught the animal after it had gone a mile or two, we, meanwhile, creeping on slowly so as not to frighten it more. Loose horses in the road make trouble. There is no one to look after them, and nine times out of ten they will go running ahead of the machine, like frightened deer, for miles. If the machine stops, they stop; if it starts, they start; it is impossible to get by. All one can do is to go on until they turn into a farmyard or down a cross-road.

The road led into Toledo, but we were told that by turning east at Perrysburg, some miles southwest of Toledo, we would have fifty miles or more of the finest road in the world, — the famous Perry's Pike.

All day long we lived in anticipation of the treat to come; at each steep hill and when struggling in the sand we mentioned Perry's Pike as the promised land. When we viewed it, we felt with Moses that the sight was sufficient.

In its day it must have been one of the wonders of the West, it is so wide and straight. In the centre is a broad, perfectly flat, raised strip of half-broken limestone. The reckless sumptuousness of such a highway in early days must have been overpowering, but with time and weather this strip of stone has worn into an infinite number of little ruts and hollows, with stones the size of cocoanuts sticking up everywhere. A trolley-line along one side of this central stretch has not improved matters.

Perry's Pike is so bad people will not use it; a road alongside the fence has been made by travel, and in dry weather this road is good, barring the pipes which cross it from oil-wells, and the many stone culverts, at each of which it is necessary to swing up onto the pike. The turns from the side road onto the pike at these culverts are pretty sharp, and in swinging up one, while going at about twenty-five miles an hour, we narrowly escaped going over the low stone wall into the ditch below. On that and one other occasion the Professor took a firmer hold of the side of the machine, but, be it said to the credit of learning, at no time did he utter an exclamation, or show the slightest sign of losing his head and jumping — as he afterwards remarked, "What's the use?"

To anyone by the roadside the danger of a smash-up seems to come and pass in an instant, — not so to the person driving the machine; to him the danger is perceptible a very appreciable length of time before the critical point is reached.

The secret of good driving lies in this early and complete appreciation of difficulties and dangers encountered. "Blind recklessness" is a most expressive phrase; it means all the words indicate, and is contra-distinguished from open-eyed or wise recklessness.

The timid man is never reckless, the wise man frequently is, the fool always; the recklessness of the last is blind; if he gets through all right he is lucky.

It is reckless to race sixty miles an hour over a highway; but the man who does it with his eyes wide open, with a perfect appreciation of all the dangers, is, in reality, less reckless than the man who blindly runs his machine, hit or miss, along the road at thirty miles an hour, — the latter leaves havoc in his train. One must have a cool, quick, and accurate appreciation of the margin of safety under all circumstances; it is the utilization of this entire margin — to the very verge — that yields the largest results in the way of rapid progress.

Every situation presents its own problem, — a problem largely mechanical, — a matter of power, speed, and obstructions; the chauffeur will win out whose perception of the conditions affecting these several factors is quickest and clearest.

One man will go down a hill, or make a safe turn at a high rate of speed, where another will land in the ditch, simply because the former overlooks nothing, while the latter does. It is not so much a matter of experience as of natural bent and adaptability. Some men can drive machines with very little experience and no instructions; others cannot, however long they try and however much they are told.

Accidents on the road are due to Defects in the road, Defects in the machine, or Defects in the driver.

American roads are bad, but not so bad that they can, with justice, be held responsible for many of the troubles attributed to them.

The roads are as they are, a practically constant, — and, for some time to come, — an unchangeable quantity. The roads are like the hills and the mountains, obstacles which must be overcome, and machines must be constructed to overcome them.

Complaints against American roads by American manufacturers of automobiles are as irrelevant to the issue as would be complaints on the part of traction-engine builders or wagon makers. Any man who makes vehicles for a given country must make them to go under the conditions — good, bad, or indifferent — which prevail in that country. In building automobiles for America or Australia, the only pertinent question is, "What are the roads of America or Australia?" not what ought they to be.

The manufacturer who finds fault with the roads should go out of the business.

Roads will be improved, but in a country so vast and sparsely settled as North America, it is not conceivable that within the next century a network of fine roads will cover the land; for generations to come there will be soft roads, sandy roads, rocky roads, hilly roads, muddy roads, — and the American automobile must be so constructed as to cover them as they are.

The manufacturer who waits for good roads everywhere should move his factory to the village of Falling Waters, and sleep in the Kaatskills.

Machines which give out on bad roads, simply because the roads are bad, are faultily constructed.

Defects in roads, to which mishaps may be fairly attributed, are only those unlooked for conditions which make trouble for all other vehicles, such as wash-outs, pit-holes, weak culverts, broken bridges, — in short, conditions which require repairs to restore the road to normal condition. The normal condition may be very bad; but whatever it is, the automobile must be constructed so as to travel thereon, else it is not adapted to that section of the country.

It may be discouraging to the driver for pleasure to find in rainy weather almost bottomless muck and mud on portions of the main travelled highway between New York and Buffalo, but that, for the present, is normal. The manufacturer may regret the condition and wish for better, but he cannot be heard to complain, and if the machine, with reasonably careful driving, gives out, it is the fault of the maker and not the roads.

It follows, therefore, that few troubles can be rightfully attributed to defects in the road, since what are commonly called defects are conditions quite normal to the country.

Fremont, August 2

It was nearly six o'clock when we arrived at Fremont. The streets were filled with people in gala attire, the militia were out, — bands playing, fire-crackers going, — a belated Fourth of July.

When we stopped for water, we casually asked a small patriot:

"What are you celebrating?"

"The second of August," was the prompt reply. I left it to the Professor to find out what had happened on the second of August, for the art of teaching is the concealment of ignorance.

With a fine assumption of his very best lecture-room manner, the Professor leaned carelessly upon the delicate indicator on the gasoline tank and began:

"That was a great day, my boy."

"Yes, sir, it was."

"And it comes once a year."

"Why, sure."

"Ahem — " in some confusion, "I mean you celebrate once a year."

"Sure, we celebrate every second of August, and it comes every year."

"Quite right, quite right; always recall with appropriate exercises the great events in your country's history." The Professor peered benignly over his glasses at the boy and continued kindly but firmly:

"Now, my boy, do you go to school?"

"Yes, sir."

"Very good. Now can you tell me why the people of Fremont celebrate the second of August?"

"Sure, it is on account of — " then a curious on-looker nudged the Professor in the ribs and began, as so many had done before, —

"Say, mister, it's none of my business — "

"Exactly," groaned the Professor; "it weighs a ton — two tons sometimes — more in the sand; it cost twelve hundred dollars, and will cost more before we are done with it. Yes, I know what you are about to say, you could buy a 'purty slick' team for that price, — in fact, a dozen nags such as that one leaning against you, — but we don't care for horses. My friend here who is spilling the water all over the machine and the small boy, once owned a horse, it kicked over the dash-board, missed his mother-in-law and hit him; horse's intention good, but aim bad, — since then he has been prejudiced against horses; it goes by gasoline — sometimes; that is not a boiler, it is the cooler — on hot days we take turns sitting on it; — explosions, — electric spark, — yes, it is queer; — man at last stop made same bright remark; no danger from explosions if you are not too near, — about a block away is safer; start by turning a crank; yes, that is queer, queerer than the other queer things; cylinder does get hot, but so do we all at times; we ought to have water jackets — that is a joke that goes with the machine; yes, it is very fast, from fifty to seventy miles per — ; 'per what?' you say; well, that depends upon the roads, — not at all, I assure you, no trouble to anticipate your inquiries by these answers — it is so seldom one meets anyone who is really interested — you can order a machine by telegraph; any more information you would like? — No! — then my friend, in return, will you tell me why you celebrate the second of August?"

"Danged if I know." And we never found out.

At Bellevue we lighted our lamps and ran to Norwalk over a very fair road, arriving a few minutes after eight. Norwalk liveries did not like automobiles, so we put the machine under a shed.

This second day's run was about one hundred and fifty miles in twelve hours and fifty-four minutes gross time; deducting stops, left nine hours and fifty-four minutes running time — an average of about fourteen and one-half miles per hour.

Ohio roads are by no means so good as Indiana. Not until we left Painesville did we find any gravel to speak of. There was not much deep sand, but roads were dry, dusty, and rough; in many localities hard clay with deep ruts and holes.

A six o'clock call and a seven o'clock breakfast gave time enough to inspect the machine.

The water-tank was leaking through a crack in the side, but not so badly that we could not go on to Cleveland, where repairs could be made more quickly. A slight pounding which had developed was finally located in the pinion of a small gear-wheel that operated the exhaust-valve.

It is sometimes by no means easy to locate a pounding in a gasoline motor, and yet it must be found and stopped. An expert from the factory once worked four days trying to locate a very loud and annoying pounding. He, of course, looked immediately at the crank- and wrist-pins, taking up what little wear was perceptible, but the pounding remained; then eccentric strap, pump, and every bearing about the motor were gone over one by one, without success; the main shaft was lifted out, fly-wheel drawn off, a new key made; the wheel drawn on again tight, all with no effect upon the hard knock which came at each explosion. At last the guess was made that possibly the piston was a trifle small for the cylinder; a new and slightly larger piston was put in and the noise ceased. It so happened that the expert had heard of one other such case, therefore he made the experiment of trying a fractionally larger piston as a last resort; imagine the predicament of the amateur, or the mechanic who had never heard of such a trouble.

There is, of course, a dull thud at each explosion; this is the natural "kick" of the engine, and is very perceptible on large single-cylinder motors; but this dull thud is very different from the hammer-like knock resulting from lost motion between the parts, and the practised ear will detect the difference at once.

The best way to find the pounding is to throw a stream of heavy lubricating oil on the bearings, one by one, until the noise is silenced for the moment. Even the piston can be reached with a flood of oil and tested.

It is not easy to tell by feeling whether a bearing on a gasoline motor is too free. The heat developed is so great that bearings are left with considerable play.

A leak in the water-tank or coils is annoying; but if facilities for permanent repair are lacking, a pint of bran or middlings from any farmer's barn, put in the water, will close the leak nine times out of ten.

From Norwalk through Wakeman and Kipton to Oberlin the road is rather poor, with but two or three redeeming stretches near Kipton. It is mostly clay, and in dry weather is hard and dusty and rough from much traffic.

Leading into Oberlin the road is covered with great broad flag-stones, which once upon a time must have presented a smooth hard surface, but now make a succession of disagreeable bumps.

Out of Elyria we made the mistake of leaving the trolley line, and for miles had to go through sand, which greatly lessened our speed, but towards Stony River the road was perfect, and we made the best time of the day.

It required some time in Cleveland to remove and repair the water-tank, cut a link out of the chain, take up the lost motion in the steering-wheel, and tighten up things generally. It was four o'clock before we were off for Painesville.

Euclid Avenue is well paved in the city, but just outside there is a bit of old plank road that is disgracefully bad. Through Wickliff, Willoughby, and Mentor the road is a smooth, hard gravel.

Arriving at Painesville a few minutes after seven, we took in gasoline, had supper, and prepared to start for Ashtabula.

It was dark, so we could not see the tires; but just before starting I gave each a sharp blow with a wrench to see if it was hard, — a sharp blow, or even a kick, tells the story much better than feeling of the tires.

One rear tire was entirely deflated. A railroad spike four and three-quarters inches long, and otherwise well proportioned, had penetrated full length. It had been picked up along the trolley line, was probably struck by the front wheel, lifted up on end so that the rear tire struck the sharp end exactly the right angle to drive the spike in lengthwise of the tread.

It was a big ragged puncture which could not be repaired on the road; there was nothing to do but stop overnight and have a tire sent out from Cleveland next day.

While waiting the next morning, we jacked up the wheel and removed the damaged tire.

It is not easy to remove quickly and put on heavy single-tube tires, and a few suggestions may not be amiss. The best tools are half-leaves of carriage springs. At any carriage shop one can get halves of broken springs. They should be sixteen or eighteen inches long, and are ready for use without forging filing or other preparation. With three such halves one man can take off a tire in fifteen or twenty minutes; two men will work a little faster; help on the road is never wanting.

Let the wheel rest on the tire with valve down; loosen all the lugs; insert thin edge of spring-leaf between rim and tire, breaking the cement and partially freeing tire; insert spring-leaf farther at a point just about opposite valve and pry tire free from rim, holding and working it free by pushing in other irons or screw-drivers, or whatever you have handy; when lugs and tire are out of the hollow of the rim for a distance of eighteen or twenty inches, it will be easy to pass the iron underneath the tire, prying up the tire until it slips over the rim, when with the hands it can be pulled off entirely; the wheel is then raised and the valve-stem carefully drawn out.

All this can be done with the wheel jacked up, but if resting on the tire as suggested, the valve-stem is protected during the efforts to loosen tire.

To put on a single-tube tire properly, the rim should be thoroughly cleaned with gasoline, and the new tire put on with shellac or cement, or with simply the lugs to hold.

Shellac can be obtained at any drugstore, is quickly brushed over both the tire and the rim, and the tire put in place — that holds very well. Cement well applied is stronger. If the rim is well covered with old cement, gasoline applied to the surface of the old cement will soften it; or with a plumber's torch the rim may be heated without injuring enamel and the cement melted, or take a cake of cement, soften it in gasoline or melt it, or even light it like a stick of sealing-wax and apply it to the rim. If hot cement is used it will be necessary to heat the rim after the tire is onto make a good job.

After the rim is prepared, insert valve-stem and the lugs near it; let the wheel down so as to rest on that part of the tire, then with the iron work the tire into the rim, beginning at each side of valve. The tire goes into place easily until the top is reached where the two irons are used to lift tire and lugs over the rim; once in rim it is often necessary to pound the tire with the flat of the iron to work the lugs into their places; by striking the tire in the direction it should go, the lugs one by one will slip into their holes; put on the nuts and the work is done.

In selecting a half-leaf of a spring, choose one the width of the springs to the machine, and carry along three or four small spring clips, for it is quite likely a spring may be broken in the course of a long run, and, if so, the half-leaf can be clipped over the break, making the broken spring as serviceable and strong for the time being as if sound.

CHAPTER 5

On to Buffalo

"GEE WHIZ!!"

From Painesville three roads led east, — the North Ridge, Middle Ridge, and South Ridge. We followed the middle road, which is said to be by far the best; it certainly is as good a gravel road as one could ask. Some miles out a turn is made to the South Ridge for Ashtabula.

There is said to be a good road out of Ashtabula; possibly there is, but we missed it at one of the numerous cross roads, and soon found ourselves wallowing through corn-fields, climbing hills, and threading valleys in the vain effort to find Girard, — a point quite out of our way, as we afterwards learned.

The Professor's bump of locality is a depression. As a passenger without serious occupation, it fell to his lot to inquire the way. This he would do very minutely, with great suavity and becoming gravity, and then with no sign of hesitation indicate invariably the wrong road. Once, after crossing a field where there were no fences to mark the highway, descending a hill we could not have mounted, and finding a stream that seemed impassable, the Professor quietly remarked, —

"That old man must have been mistaken regarding the road; yet he had lived on that corner forty years. Strange how little some people know about their surroundings!"

"But are you sure he said the first turn to the left?"

"He said the first turn, but whether to the left or right I cannot now say. It must have been to the right."

"But, my dear Professor, you said to the left."

"Well, we were going pretty fast when we came to the four corners, and something had to be said, and said quickly. I notice that on an automobile decision is more important than accuracy. After being hauled over the country for three days, I have made up my mind that automobiles are driven upon the hypothesis that it is better to lose the road, lose life, lose anything than lose time, therefore, when you ask me which way to turn, you will get an immediate, if not an accurate, response; besides, there is a bridge ahead, a little village across the stream, so the road leads somewhere."

Now and then the Professor would jump out to assist some female in distress with her horse; at first it was a matter of gallantry, then a duty, then a burden. Towards the last it used to delight him to see people frantically turning into lanes, fields, anywhere to get out of the way.

The horse is a factor to be considered — and placated. He is in possession and cannot be forcibly ejected, — a sort of terre-tenant; such title as he has must be respected.

After wrestling with an unusually notional beast, to the great disorder of clothing and temper, the Professor said, —

"The brain of the horse is small; it is an animal of little sense and great timidity, but it knows more than most people who attempt to drive."

In reality horses are seldom driven; they generally go as they please, with now and then a hint as to which corner to turn. Nine times out of ten it is the driven horse that makes trouble for owners of automobiles. The drunken driver never has any trouble; his horses do not stop, turn about, or shy into the ditch; the man asleep on the box is perfectly safe; his horse ambles on, minding its own business, giving a full half of the road to the approaching machine. It is the man, who, on catching sight of the automobile, nervously gathers up his reins, grabs his whip, and pulls and jerks, who makes his own troubles; he is searching for trouble, expects it, and is disappointed if he gets by without it. Nine times out of ten it is the driver who really frightens the horse. A country plug, jogging quietly along, quite unterrified, may be roused to unwonted capers by the person behind.

Some take the antics of their horses quite philosophically. One old farmer, whose wheezy nag tried to climb the fence, called out, —

"Gee whiz! I wish you fellers would come this way every day; the old hoss hasn't showed so much ginger for ten year."

Another, carrying just a little more of the wine of the country than his legs could bear, stood up unsteadily in his wagon and shouted, —

"If you (hic) come around these pa-arts again with that thres-in' ma-a-chine, I'll have the law on you, — d'ye hear?"

The personal equation is everything on the road, as elsewhere.

It is quite idle to expect skill, courage, or common sense from the great majority of drivers. They get along very well so long as nothing happens, but in emergencies they are helpless, because they have never had experience in emergencies. The man who has driven horses all his life is frequently as helpless under unusual conditions as the novice. Few drivers know when and how to use the whip to prevent a runaway or a smash-up.

With the exception of professional and a few amateur whips, no one is ever taught how to drive. Most persons who ride — even country boys — are given many useful hints, lessons, and demonstrations; but it seems to be assumed that driving is a natural acquirement.

As a matter of fact, it is much more important to be taught how to drive than how to ride. A horse in front of a vehicle can do all the mean things a horse under a saddle can do, and more; and it is far more difficult to handle an animal in shafts by means of long reins and a whip.

If people knew half as much about horses as they think they do, there would be no mishaps; if horses were half as nervous as they are supposed to be, the accidents would be innumerable.

The truth is, the horse does very well if managed with a little common sense, skill, and coolness.

As a matter of law, the automobile is a vehicle, and has precisely the same rights on the highway that a bicycle or a carriage has. The horse has no monopoly of the highway, it enjoys no especial privileges, but must share the road with all other vehicles. Furthermore, the law makes it the business of the horse to get accustomed to strange sights and behave itself This duty has been onerous the last few years; the bicycle, the traction engine, and the trolley have come along in quick succession; the automobile is about the last straw.

Until the horse is accustomed to the machine, it is the duty — by law and common sense — of the automobile driver to take great care in passing; the care being measured by the possibility of an accident.

The sympathy of every chauffeur must be entirely with the driver of the horse. Automobiles are not so numerous in this country that they may be looked for at every turn, and one cannot but feel for the man or woman who, while driving, sees one coming down the road. The best of drivers feel panicky, while women and children are terror-stricken.

It is no uncommon sight to see people jump out of their carriages or drive into fields or lanes, anywhere, to get out of the way. In localities where machines have been driven recklessly, men and women, though dressed in their best, frequently jump out in the mud as soon as an automobile comes in sight, and long before the chauffeur has an opportunity to show that he will exercise caution in approaching. All this is wrong and creates an amount of ill-feeling hard to overcome.

If one is driving along a fine road at twenty or thirty miles an hour, it is, of course, a relief to see coming vehicles turn in somewhere; but it ought not to be necessary for them to do so. Often people like to turn to one side for the sake of seeing the machine go by at full speed; but if they do not wish to, the automobile should be so driven as to pass with safety.

On country roads there is but one way to pass horses without risk, and that is let the horses pass the machine.

In cities horses give very little trouble; in the country they give no end of trouble; they are a very great drawback to the pleasure of automobiling. Horses that behave well in the city are often the very worst in the country, so susceptible is the animal to environment.

On narrow country roads three out of five will behave badly, and unless the outward signs are unmistakable, it is never safe to assume one is meeting an old plug, — even the plug sometimes jumps the ditch.

The safe, the prudent, the courteous thing to do is to stop and let the driver drive or lead his horse by; if a child or woman is driving, get out and lead the horse.

By stopping the machine most horses can be gotten by without much trouble. Even though the driver motions to come on, it is seldom safe to do so; for of all horses the one that is brought to a stand-still in front of a machine is surest to shy, turn, or bolt when the machine starts up to pass. If one is going to pass a horse without stopping, it is safer to do so quickly, — the more quickly the better; but that is taking great chances.

Whenever a horse, whether driven or hitched, shows fright, a loud, sharp "Whoa!" from the chauffeur will steady the animal. The voice from the machine, if sharp and peremptory, is much more effective than any amount of talking from the carriage.

Much of the prejudice against automobiles is due to the fact that machines are driven with entire disregard for the feelings and rights of horse owners; in short, the highway is monopolized to the exclusion of the public. The prejudice thus created is manifested in many ways that are disagreeable to the chauffeur and his friends.

The trouble is not in excessive speed, and speed ordinances will not remedy the trouble. A machine may be driven as recklessly at ten or twelve miles an hour as at thirty. In a given distance more horses can be frightened by a slow machine than a fast. It is all in the manner of driving.

Speed is a matter of temperament. In England, the people and local boards cannot adopt measures stringent enough to prevent speeding; in Ireland, the people and local authorities line the highways, urging the chauffeur to let his machine out; in America, we are suspended between English prudence and repression on the one side and Irish impulsiveness and recklessness on the other.

The Englishman will not budge; the Irishman cries, "Let her go."

Speaking of the future of the automobile, the Professor said, —

"Cupid will never use the automobile, the little god is too conservative; fancy the dainty sprite with oil-can and waste instead of bow and arrow. I can see him with smut on the end of his mischievous nose and grease on the seat of the place where his trousers ought to be. What a picture he would make in overalls and jumper, leather jacket and cap; he could not use dart or arrow, at best he could only run the machine hither and thither bunting people into love — knocking them senseless, which is perhaps the same thing. No, Cupid will never use the automobile. Imagine Aphrodite in goggles, clothed in dust, her fair skin red from sunburn and glistening with cold cream; nightmare of a mechanical age, avaunt!

"The chariots of High Olympus were never greased, they used no gasoline, the clouds we see about them are condensed zephyrs and not dust. Omniscient Jove never used a monkey-wrench, never sought the elusive spark, never blew up a four-inch tire with a half-inch pump. Even if the automobile could surmount the grades, it would never be popular on Olympian heights. Mercury might use it to visit Vulcan, but he would never go far from the shop.

"As for conditions here on earth, why should a young woman go riding with a man whose hands, arms, and attention are entirely taken up with wheels, levers, and oil-cups? He can't even press her foot without running the risk of stopping the machine by releasing some clutch; if he moves his knees a hair's-breadth in her direction it does something to the mechanism; if he looks her way they are into the ditch; if she attempts to kiss him his goggles prevent; his sighs are lost in the muffler and hers in the exhaust; nothing but dire disaster will bring an automobile courtship to a happy termination; as long as the machine goes love-making is quite out of the question.

"Dobbin, dear old secretive Dobbin, what difference does it make to you whether you feel the guiding hand or not? You know when the courtship begins, the brisk drives about town to all points of interest, to the pond, the poorhouse, and the cemetery; you know how the courtship progresses, the long drives in the country, the idling along untravelled roads and woodland ways, the moonlight nights and misty meadows; you know when your stops to nibble by the wayside will not be noticed, and you alone know when it is time to get the young couple home; you know, alas! when the courtship—blissful period of loitering for you—is ended and when the marriage is made, by the tighter rein, the sharper word, and the occasional swish of the whip. Ah, Dobbin, you and I—" The Professor was becoming indiscreet.

"What do you know about love-making, Professor?"

"My dear fellow, it is the province of learning to know everything and practise nothing."

"But Dobbin—"

"We all have had our Dobbins."

For some miles the road out of Erie was soft, dusty, narrow, and poor —by no means fit for the proposed Erie-Buffalo race. About fifteen miles out there is a sharp turn to the left and down a steep incline with a ravine and stream below on the right, — a dangerous turn at twenty miles an hour, to say nothing of forty or fifty.

There is nothing to indicate that the road drops so suddenly after making the turn, and we were bowling along at top speed; a wagon coming around the corner threw us well to the outside, so that the margin of safety was reduced to a minimum, even if the turn were an easy one.

As we swung around the corner well over to the edge of the ravine, we saw the grade we had to make. Nothing but a succession of small rain gullies in the road saved us from going down the bank. By so steering as to drop the skidding wheels on the outside into each gully, the sliding of the machine received a series of violent checks and we missed the brink of the ravine by a few inches.

A layman in the Professor's place would have jumped; but he, good man, looked upon his escape as one of the incidents of automobile travel.

"When I accepted your invitation, my dear fellow, I expected something beyond the ordinary. I have not been disappointed."

It was a wonder the driving-wheels were not dished by the violent side strains, but they were not even sprung. These wheels were of wire tangential spokes; they do not look so well as the smart, heavy, substantial wooden wheels one sees on nearly all imported machines and on some American.

The sense of proportion between parts is sadly outraged by spindle-wire wheels supporting the massive frame-work and body of an automobile; however strong they may be in reality, architecturally they are quite unfit, and no doubt the wooden wheel will come more and more into general use.

A wooden wheel with the best of hickory spokes possesses an elasticity entirely foreign to the rigid wire wheel, but good hickory wheels are rare; paint hides a multitude of sins when spread over wood; and inferior wooden wheels are not at all to be relied upon.

Soon we begin to catch glimpses of Lake Erie through the trees and between the hills, just a blue expanse of water shining in the morning sun, a sapphire set in the dull brown gold of woods and fields. Farther on we come out upon the bluffs overlooking the lake and see the smoke and grime of Buffalo far across. What a blot on a view so beautiful!

"Civilization," said the Professor, "is the subjection of nature. In the civilization of Athens nature was subdued to the ends of beauty; in the civilization of America nature is subdued to the ends of usefulness; in every civilization nature is of secondary importance, it is but a means to an end. Nature and the savage, like little children, go hand in hand, the one the complement of the other; but the savage grows and grows, while nature remains ever a child, to sink subservient at last to its early play-mate. Just now we in this country are treating nature with great harshness, making of her a drudge and a slave; her pretty hands are soiled, her clean face covered with soot, her clothing tattered and torn. Some day, we as a nation will tire of playing the taskmaster and will treat the playmate of man's infancy and youth with more consideration; we will adorn and not disfigure her, love and not ignore her, place her on a throne beside us, make her queen to our kingship."

"Professor, the automobile hardly falls in with your notions."

"On the contrary, the automobile is the one absolutely fit conveyance for America. It is a noisy, dirty, mechanical contrivance, capable of great speed; it is the only vehicle in which one could approach that distant smudge on the landscape with any sense of the eternal fitness of things. A coach and four would be as far behind the times on this highway as a birch-bark canoe on yonder lake. In America an automobile is beautiful because it is in perfect harmony with the spirit of the age and country; it is twin brother to the trolley; train, trolley, and automobile may travel side by side as members of one family, late offsprings of man's ingenuity."

"But you would not call them things of beauty?"

"Yes and no; beauty is so largely relative that one cannot pronounce hideous anything that is a logical and legitimate development. Considered in the light of things the world pronounces beautiful, there are no more hideous monstrosities on the face of the earth than train, trolley, and automobile; but each generation has its own standard of beauty, though it seldom confesses it. We say and actually persuade ourselves that we admire the Parthenon; in reality we admire the mammoth factory and the thirty-story office building. Strive as we may to deceive ourselves by loud protestations, our standards are not the standards of old. We like best the things we have; we may call things ugly, but we think them beautiful, for they are part of us, — and the automobile fits into our surroundings like a pocket in a coat. We may turn up our noses at it or away from it, as the case may be, but none the less it is the perambulator of the twentieth century."

It was exactly one o'clock when we pulled up near the City Hall. Total time from Erie: five hours and fifty minutes; actual running time five hours; distance by road about ninety-four miles.

CHAPTER 6

Buffalo

THE MIDWAY

Housing the machine in a convenient and well-appointed stable for automobiles, we were reminded of the fact that we had arrived in Buffalo at no ordinary time, by a charge of three dollars per night for storage, with everything else extra. But was it not the Exposition we had come to see? and are not Expositions proverbially expensive — to promoters and stockholders as well as visitors?

Then, too, the hotels of Buffalo had expected so much and were so woefully disappointed. Vast arrays of figures had been compiled showing that within a radius of four hundred miles of Buffalo lived all the people in the United States who were worth knowing. The statistics were not without their foundation in fact, but therein lay the weakness of the entire scheme so far as hotels were concerned; people lived so near they could leave home in the morning with a boiled egg and a sandwich, see the Exposition and get back at night. Travellers passing through would stop over during the day and evening, then go their way on a midnight train, — it was cheaper to ride in a Pullman than stay in Buffalo.

We might have taken rooms at Rochester, running back and forth each day in the machine, — though Rochester was by no means beyond the zone of exorbitant charges. Notions of value become very much congested within a radius of two or three hundred miles of any great Exposition.

The Exposition was well worth seeing in parts by day and as a whole by night. The electrical display at night was a triumph of engineering skill and architectural arrangement. It was the falls of Niagara turned into stars, the mist of the mighty cascade crystallized into jewels, a brilliant crown to man's triumph over the forces of nature.

It was a wonderful and never-to-be-forgotten sight to sit by the waters at night, as the shadows were folding the buildings in their soft embrace, and see the first faint twinklings of the thousands upon thousands of lights as the great current of electricity was turned slowly on; and then to see the lights grow in strength until the entire grounds were bathed in suffused radiance, — that was as wonderful a sight as the world of electricity has yet witnessed, and it was well worth crossing an ocean to see; it was the one conspicuous success, the one memorable feature of the Exposition, and compared with it all exhibits and scenes by day were tame and insipid.

From time immemorial it has been the special province of the preacher to take the children to the circus and the side show; for the children must go, and who so fit to take them as the preacher? After all, is not the sawdust ring with its strange people, its giants, fairies, hobgoblins, and clowns, a fairy land, not really real, and therefore no more wicked than fairy land? Do they not fly by night? are they not children of space? the enormous tents spring up like mushrooms, to last a day; for a few short hours, there is a medley of strange sounds, — a blare of trumpets, the roar of strange beasts, the ring of strange voices, the crackling of whips; there are prancing steeds and figures in costumes curious, — then, flapping of canvas, creaking of poles, and all is silent. Of course it is not real, and everyone may go. The circus has no annals, knows no gossip, presents no problems; it is without morals and therefore not immoral. It is the one joyous amusement that is not above, but quite outside the pale of criticism and discussion. Therefore, why should not the preacher go and take the children?

But the Midway. Ah! the Midway, that is quite a different matter; but still the preacher goes, — leaving the children at home.

Learning is ever curious. The Professor, after walking patiently through several of the buildings and admiring impartially sections of trees from Cuba and plates of apples from Wyoming, modestly expressed a desire for some relaxation.

"The Midway is something more than a feature, it is an element. It is the laugh that follows the tears; the joke that relieves the tension; the Greeks invariably produced a comedy with their tragedies; human nature demands relaxation; to appreciate the serious, the humorous is absolutely essential. If the Midway were not on the grounds the people would find it outside. Capacity for serious contemplation differs with different peoples and in different ages, — under Cromwell it was at a maximum, under Charles II it was at a minimum; the Puritans suppressed the laughter of a nation; it broke out in ridicule that discriminated not between sacred and profane. The tension of our age is such that diversions must recur quickly. The next great Exposition may require two Midways, or three or four for the convenience of the people. You can't get a Midway any too near the anthropological and ethnological sections; a cinematograph might be operated as an adjunct to the Fine Arts building; a hula-hula dancer would relieve the monotony of a succession of big pumpkins and prize squashes."

At that moment the Professor became interested in the strange procession entering the streets of Cairo, and we followed. Before he got out it cost him fifty cents to learn his name, a quarter for his fortune, ten cents for his horoscope, and sundry amounts for gems, jewels, and souvenirs of the Orient.

Through his best hexameter spectacles he surveyed the dark-eyed daughter of the Nile who was telling his fortune with a strong Irish accent; all went smoothly until the prophetess happened to see the Professor's sunburnt nose, fiery red from the four days' run in wind and rain, and said warningly:

"You are too fond of good eating and drinking; you drink too much, and unless you are more temperate you will die in twenty years." That was too much for the Professor, whose occasional glass of beer—a habit left over from his student days—would not discolor the nose of a humming-bird.

There were no end of illusions, mysteries, and deceptions. The greatest mystery of all was the eager desire of the people to be deceived, and their bitter and outspoken disappointment when they were not. As the Professor remarked:

"There never has been but one real American, and that was Phineas T. Barnum. He was the genuine product of his country and his times, — native ore without foreign dross. He knew the American people as no man before or since has known them; he knew what the American people wanted, and gave it to them in large unadulterated doses, — humbug."

Tuesday morning was spent in giving the machine a thorough inspection, some lost motion in the eccentric was taken up, every nut and screw tightened, and the cylinder and intake mechanism washed out with gasoline.

It is a good plan to clean out the cylinder with gasoline once each week or ten days; it is not necessary, but the piston moves with much greater freedom and the compression is better.

However good the cylinder oil used, after six or eight days' hard and continuous running there is more or less residuum; in the very nature of things there must be from the consumption of about a pint of oil to every hundred miles.

Many use kerosene to clean cylinders, but gasoline has its advantages; kerosene is excellent for all other bearings. especially where there may be rust, as on the chain; but kerosene is in itself a low grade oil, and the object in cleaning the cylinder is to cut out all the oil and leave it bright and dry ready for a supply of fresh oil.

After putting in the gasoline, the cylinder and every bearing which the gasoline has touched should be thoroughly lubricated before starting.

Lubrication is of vital importance, and the oil used makes all the difference in the world.

Many makers of machines have adopted the bad practice of putting up oil in cans under their own brands, and charging, of course, two prices per gallon. The price is of comparatively little consequence, though an item; for it does not matter so much whether one pays fifty cents or a dollar a gallon, so long as the best oil is obtained; the pernicious feature of the practice lies in wrapping the oil in mystery, like a patent medicine, — "Smith's Cylinder Oil" and "Jones's Patent Pain-Killer" being in one and the same category. Then they warn — patent medicine methods again — purchasers of machines that their particular brand of oil must be used to insure best results.

The one sure result is that the average user who knows nothing about lubricating oils is kept in a state of frantic anxiety lest his can of oil runs low at a time and place where he cannot get more of the patent brand.

Every manufacturer should embody in the directions for caring for the machine information concerning all the standard oils that can be found in most cities, and recommend the use of as many different brands as possible.

Machine oil can be found in almost any country village, or at any mill, factory, or power-house along the road; it is the cylinder oil that requires fore-thought and attention.

Beware of steam-cylinder oil and all heavy and gummy oils. Rub a little of any oil that is offered between the fingers until it disappears, — the better the oil the longer you can rub it. If it leaves a gummy or sticky feeling, do not use; but if it rubs away thin and oily, it is probably good. Of course the oiliest of oils are animal fats. good lard, and genuine sperm; but they work down very thin and run away, and genuine sperm oil is almost an unknown quantity. Lard can be obtained at every farmhouse, and may be used, if necessary, on bearings.

In an emergency, olive oil and probably cotton-seed oil may be used in the cylinder. Olive oil is a fine lubricant, and is used largely in the Italian and Spanish navies.

Many special brands are probably good oils and safe to use, but there is no need of staking one's trip upon any particular brand.

All good steam-cylinder oils contain animal oil to make them adhere to the side of the cylinder; a pure mineral oil would be washed away by the steam and water.

To illustrate the action of oils and water, take a clean bottle, put in a little pure mineral oil, add some water, and shake hard; the oil will rise to the top of the water in little globules without adhering at all to the sides of the bottle; in short, the bottle is not lubricated. Instead of a pure mineral oil put in any steam-cylinder oil which is a compound of mineral and animal; and as the bottle is shaken the oil adheres to the glass, covering the entire inner surface with a film that the water will not rinse off.

As there is supposed—erroneously—to be no moisture in the cylinder of a gas-engine, the use of any animal oil is said to be unnecessary; as there is moisture in the cylinder of a steam-engine, some animal oil is absolutely essential in the cylinder oil.

For the lubrication of chains and all parts exposed to the weather, compounds of oil or grease which contain a liberal amount of animal fat are better. Rain and the splash of mud and water will wash off mineral oil as fast as it can be applied; in fact, under adverse weather conditions it does not lubricate at all; the addition of animal fat makes the compound stick.

Graphite and mica are both good chain lubricants, but if mixed with a pure mineral base, such as vaseline, they will wash off in mud and water.

Before putting on a chain, it is a good thing to dip it in melted tallow and then grease it thoroughly from time to time with a graphite compound of vaseline and animal fat.

One does not expect perfection in a machine, but there is not an automobile made, according to the reports of users, which does not develop many crudities and imperfections in construction which could be avoided by care and conscientious work in the factory, — crudities and imperfections which customers and users have complained of time and time again, but without avail.

At best the automobile is a complicated and difficult machine in the hands of the amateur, and so far it has been made almost impossible by its poor construction. With good construction there will be troubles enough in operation, but at the present time ninety per cent of the stops and difficulties are due to defective construction.

As the machine comes it looks so well, it inspires unbounded confidence, but the first time it is seen in undress, with the carriage part off, the machinery laid bare, the heart sinks, and one's confidence oozes out.

Parts are twisted, bent, and hammered to get them into place, bearings are filed to make them fit, bolts and screws are weak and loose, nuts gone for the want of cotter-pins; it is as if apprentice blacksmiths had spent their idle moments in constructing a machine.

The carriage work is hopelessly bad. The building of carriages is a long-established industry, employing hundreds of thousands of hands and millions of capital, and yet in the entire United States there are scarcely a dozen builders of really fine, substantial, and durable vehicles. Yet every cross-road maker of automobiles thinks that if he can only get his motor to go, the carpenter next door can do his woodwork. The result is cheap stock springs, clips, irons, bodies, cushions, tops, etc., are bought and put over the motor. The use of aluminum bodies and more metal work generally is helping things somewhat; not that aluminum and metal work are necessarily better than wood, but it prevents the unnatural union of the light wood bodies, designed for cheap horse-vehicles, with a motor. The best French makers do not build their bodies, but leave that part to skilled carriage builders.

CHAPTER 7

Buffalo to Canandaigua

BEWARE OF THE COUNTRY MECHANIC

The five hundred and sixty-odd miles to Buffalo had been covered with no trouble that delayed us for more than an hour, but our troubles were about to begin.

The Professor had still a few days to waste frivolously, so he said he would ride a little farther, possibly as far as Albany. However, it was not our intention to hurry, but rather take it easily, stopping by the way, as the mood — or our friends — seized us.

It rained all the afternoon of Tuesday, about all night, and was raining steadily when we turned off Main Street into Genesee with Batavia thirty-eight miles straight away. We fully expected to reach there in time for luncheon; in fact, word had been sent ahead that we would "come in," like a circus, about twelve, and friends were on the lookout, — it was four o'clock when we reached town.

The road is good, gravel nearly every rod, but the steady rain had softened the surface to the depth of about two inches, and the water, sand, and gravel were splashed in showers and sheets by the wheels into and through every exposed part of the mechanism. Soon the explosions became irregular, and we found the cams operating the sparker literally plastered over with mud, so that the parts that should slide and work with great smoothness and rapidity would not operate at all. This happened about every four or five miles. This mechanism on this particular machine was so constructed and situated as to catch and hold mud, and the fine grit worked in, causing irregularities in the action. This trouble we could count upon as long as the road was wet; after noon, when the sun came out and the road began to dry, we had less trouble.

When about half-way to Batavia the spark began to show blue; the reserve set of dry batteries was put in use, but it gave no better results. Apparently there was either a short circuit, or the batteries were used up; the bad showing of the reserve set puzzled us; every connection was examined and tightened. The wiring of the carriage was so exposed to the weather that it was found completely saturated in places with oil and covered with mud. The rubber insulation had been badly disintegrated wherever oil had dropped on it. The wires were cleaned as thoroughly as possible and separated wherever the insulation seemed poor. The loss of current was probably at the sparking coil; the mud had so covered the end where the binding parts project as to practically join them by a wet connection. Cleaning this off and protecting the binding parts with insulating tape we managed to get on, the spark being by no means strong, and the reserve battery for some reason weak.

If we had had a small buzzer, such as is sold for a song at every electrical store, to say nothing of a pocket voltmeter, we would have discovered in a moment that the reserve battery contained one dead cell, the resistance of which made the other cells useless At Batavia we tested them out with an ordinary electric bell, discovering at once the dead cell.

After both batteries are so exhausted that the spark is weak, the current from both sets can be turned on at the same time in two ways; by linking the cells in multiples, — that is, side by side, or in series, — tandem.

The current from cells in multiples is increased in volume but not in force, and gives a fat spark; the current from cells in series is doubled in force and gives a long blue hot spark. Both sparks, if the cells are fresh, will burn the points, though giving much better explosions.

As the batteries weaken, first connect them in multiples, then, as they weaken still more, in series.

Always carry a roll of insulating tape, or on a pinch bicycle tire-tape will do very well. Wrap carefully every joint, and the binding-posts of the cells for the tape will hold as against vibration when the little. binding-screws will not. In short, use the tape freely to insulate, protect, and support the wires and all connections.

If the machine is wired with light and poorly insulated wire, it is but a question of time when the wiring must be done over again.

When we pulled up in Batavia at an electrician's for repairs, the Professor was a sight — and also tired. The good man had floundered about in the mud until he was picturesquely covered. At the outset he was disposed to take all difficulties philosophically.

"I should regret exceedingly," he remarked at our first involuntary stop, "to return from this altogether extraordinary trip without seeing the automobile under adverse conditions. Our experiences in the sand were no fault of the machine; the responsibility rested with us for placing it in a predicament from which it could not extricate itself, and if, in the heat of the moment and the sand, I said anything derogatory to the faithful machine, I express my regrets. Now, it seems, I shall have the pleasure of observing some of the eccentricities of the horseless carriage. What seems to be the matter?" and the Professor peered vaguely underneath.

"Something wrong with the spark."

"Bless me! Can you fix it?"

"I think so. Now, if you will be good enough to turn that crank."

"With pleasure. What an extraordinary piece of mechanism."

"A little faster."

"The momentum — "

"A little faster."

"Very heavy fly-wheel — "

"Just a little faster."

"Friction — mechanics — overcome — "

"Now as hard as you can, Professor."

"Exercise, muscle, but hard work. The spark, — is it there? Whew!" and the Professor stopped, exhausted.

It was the repetition of those experiences that sobered the Professor and led him to speak of his work at home, which he feared he was neglecting. At the last stop he stood in a pool of water and turned the crank without saying anything that would bear repetition.

While touring, look out for glass, nails, and the country mechanic, — of the three, the mechanic can do the largest amount of damage in a given time. His well-meant efforts may wreck you; his mistakes are sure to. The average mechanic along the route is a veritable bull in a china shop, — once inside your machine, and you are done for. He knows it all, and more too. He once lived next to a man who owned a naphtha launch; hence his expert knowledge; or he knew someone who was blown up by gasoline, therefore he is qualified. Look out for him; his look of intelligence is deception itself. His readiness with hammer and file means destruction; if he once gets at the machine, give it to him as a reward and a revenge for his misdirected energy, and save time by walking.

Even the men from the factory make sad mistakes; they may locate troubles, but in repairing they will forget, and leave off more things than the floor will hold.

At Batavia we put in new batteries, repacked the pump, covered the coil with patent leather, so that neither oil nor water could affect it, and put on a new chain. Without saying a word, the bright and too willing mechanic who was assisting, mainly by looking on, took the new chain into his shop and cut off a link. A wanton act done because he "thought the chain a little too long," and not discovered until the machine had been cramped together, every strut and reach shortened to get the chain in place; meanwhile the factory was being vigorously blamed for sending out chains too short. During it all the mechanic was discreetly silent, but the new link on the vise in the shop betrayed him after the harm was done.

The run from Batavia to Canandaigua was made over roads that are well-nigh perfect most of the way, but the machine was not working well, the chain being too short. Going up stiff grades it was apparent something was wrong, for while the motor worked freely the carriage dragged.

On the level and down grade everything went smoothly, but at every up grade the friction and waste of power were apparent. Inspection time and again showed everything clear, and it was not until late in the afternoon the cause of the trouble was discovered. A tell-tale mark on the surface of the fly-wheel showed friction against something, and we found that while the wheel ran freely if we were out of the machine, with the load in, and especially on up grades with the chain drawing the framework closer to the running gear, the rim of the wheel just grazed a bolt-head in a small brace underneath, thereby producing the peculiar grating noise we had heard and materially checking the motor. The shortening of the struts and reaches to admit the short chain had done all this. As the chain had stretched a little, we were able to lengthen slightly the struts so as to give a little more clearance; it was also possible to shift the brace about a quarter of an inch, and the machine once more ran freely under all conditions.

Within twenty miles of Canandaigua the country is quite rolling and many of the hills steep. Twice we were obliged to get out and let the machine mount the grades, which it did; but it was apparent that for the hills and mountains of New York the gearing was too high.

On hard roads in a level country high gearing is all well enough, and a high average speed can be maintained, but where the roads are soft or the country rolling, a high gear may mean a very material disadvantage in the long run.

It is of little use to be able to run thirty or forty miles on the level if at every grade or soft spot it is necessary to throw in the hill-climbing gear, thereby reducing the speed to from four to six miles per hour; the result-ing average is low. A carriage that will take the hills and levels of New York at the uniform speed of fifteen miles an hour will finish far ahead of one that is compelled to use low gears at every grade, even though the latter easily makes thirty or forty miles on the level.

The machine we were using had but two sets of gears, — a slow and a fast. All intermediate speeds were obtained by throttling the engine. The engine was easily governed, and on the level any speed from the lowest to the maximum could be obtained without juggling with the clutches; but on bad roads and in hilly localities intermediate gears are required if one is to get the best results out of a motor. As the gasoline motor devel-ops its highest efficiency when it is running at full speed, there should be enough intermediate gears so the maximum speed may be maintained under varying conditions. As the road gets heavy or the grades steep, the drop is made from one gear down to another; but at all times and under all conditions — if there are enough intermediate gears — the machine is being driven with the motor running fast.

With only two gears where roads or grades are such that the high gear cannot be used, there is nothing to do but drop to the low, — from thirty miles an hour to five or six, — and the engine runs as if it had no load at all. American roads especially demand intermediate gears if best results are to be attained, the conditions change so from mile to mile.

Foreign machines are equipped with from three to five speed-changing gears in addition to the spark control, and many also have throttles for governing the speed of the engine.

Going at full speed down a long hill about two miles out of Can-andaigua, we discovered that neither power nor brakes had any control over the machine. The large set-screws holding the two halves of the rear-axle in the differential gears had worked loose and the right half was steadily working out. As both brakes operated through the differential, both were useless, and the machine was beyond control. An obstacle or a bad turn at the bottom meant disaster; happily the hill terminated in a level stretch of softer road, which checked the speed and the machine came slowly to a stop.

The sensation of rushing down hill with power and brakes absolutely detached is peculiar and exhilarating. It is quite like coasting or tobog-ganing; the excitement is in proportion to the risk; the chance of safety lies in a clear road; for the time being the machine is a huge projectile, a flying mass, a ton of metal rushing through space; there is no sensation of fear, not a tremor of the nerves, but one becomes for the moment exceedingly alert, with instantaneous comprehension of the character of the road; every rut, stone, and curve are seen and appreciated; the possibility of collision is understood, and every danger is present in the mind, and with it all the thrill of excitement which ever accompanies risk.

During the entire descent the Professor was in blissful ignorance of the loss of control. To him the hill was like many another that we had taken at top speed; but when he saw the rear wheel far out from the carriage with only about twelve inches of axle holding in the sleeve, and understood the loss of control through both chain and brakes, his imagination began to work, and he thought of everything that could have happened and many things that could not, but he remarked philosophically, —

"Fear is entirely a creature of the imagination. We are not afraid of what will happen, but of what may. We are all cowards until confronted with danger; most men are heroes in emergencies."

Detaching a lamp from the front of the carriage, repairs were made. A block of wood and a fence rail made a good jack; the gear case was opened up, the axle driven home, and the set-screws turned down tight; but it was only too apparent that the screws would work loose again.

The next morning we pulled out both halves of the axle and found the key-ways worn so there was a very perceptible play. As the keys were supposed to hold the gears tight and the set-screws were only for the purpose of keeping the axle from working out, it was idle to expect the screws to hold fast so long as the keys were loose in the ways; the slight play of the gears upon the axles would soon loosen screws, in fact, both were found loose, although tightened up only the evening before.

As it had become apparent that the machine was geared too high for the hills of New York, it seemed better to send it into the shop for such changes as were necessary, rather than spend the time necessary to make them in the one small machine shop at Canandaigua.

Furthermore the Professor's vacation was drawing to a close; he had given himself not to exceed ten days, eight had elapsed.

"I feel that I have exhausted the possibilities and eccentricities of automobiling; there is nothing more to learn; if there is anything more, I do not care to know it. I am inclined to accept the experience of last night as a warning; as the fellow who was blown up with dynamite said when he came down, 'to repeat the experiment would be no novelty.'"

And so the machine was loaded on the cars, side-tracked on the way, and it was many a day before another start could be made from Buffalo.

It cannot be too often repeated that it is a mistake to ever lose sight of one's machine during a tour; it is a mistake to leave it in a machine shop for repairs; it is a mistake to even return it to the place of its creation; for you may be quite sure that things will be left undone that should be done, and things done that should not be done.

It requires days and weeks to become acquainted with all the peculiarities and weaknesses of an automobile, to know its strong points and rely upon them, to appreciate its failings and be tender towards them. After you have become acquainted, do not risk the friendship by letting the capricious thing out of your sight. It is so fickle that it forms wanton attachments for everyone it meets, — for urchins, idlers, loafers, mechanics, permits them all sorts of familiarities, so that when, like a truant, it comes wandering back, it is no longer the same, but a new creature, which you must learn again to know.

It is monotonously lonesome running an automobile across country alone; the record-breaker may enjoy it, but the civilized man does not; man is a gregarious animal, especially in his sports; one must have an audience, if an audience of only one.

The return of the Professor made it necessary to find someone else. There was but one who could go, but she had most emphatically refused; did not care for the dust and dirt, did not care for the curious crowds, did not care to go fast, did not care to go at all. To overcome these apparently insurmountable objections, a semi-binding pledge was made to not run more than ten or twelve miles per hour, and not more than thirty or forty miles per day, — promises so obviously impossible of fulfilment on the part of any chauffeur that they were not binding in law. We started out well within bounds, making but little over forty miles the first day; we wound up with a glorious run of one hundred and forty miles the last day, covering the Old Sarnia gravel out of London, Ontario, at top speed for nearly seventy miles.

For five weeks to a day we wandered over the eastern country at our own sweet will, not a care, not a responsibility, — days without seeing newspapers, finding mail and telegrams at infrequent intervals, but much of the time lost to the world of friends and acquaintances.

Touring on an automobile differs from coaching, posting, railroading, from every known means of locomotion, in that you are really lost to the world. In coaching or posting, one knows with reasonable certainty the places that can be made; the itinerary is laid out in advance, and if departed from, friends can be notified by wire, so that letters and telegrams may be forwarded.

With an automobile all is different. The vagaries of the machine upset every itinerary. You do not know where you will stop, because you cannot tell when you may stop. If one has in mind a certain place, the machine may never reach it, or, arriving, the road and the day may be so fine you are irresistibly impelled to keep on. The very thought that letters are to be at a certain place at a certain date is a bore, it limits your progress, fetters your will, and curbs your inclinations. One hears of places of interest off the chosen route; the temptation to see them is strong exactly in proportion to the assurances given that you will go elsewhere.

The automobile is lawless; it chafes under restraint; will follow neither advice nor directions. Tell it to go this way, it is sure to go that; to turn the second corner to the right, it will take the first to the left; to go to one city, it prefers another; to avoid a certain road, it selects that above all others.

It is a grievous error to tell friends you are coming; it puts them to no end of inconvenience; for days they expect you and you do not come; their feeling of relief that you did not come is destroyed by your appearance.

The day we were expected at a friend's summer home at the sea-side we spent with the Shakers in the valley of Lebanon, waiting for a new steering-head. Telegrams of concern and consolation reached us in our retreat, but those who expected us were none the less inconvenienced.

Then, too, what business have the dusty, grimy, veiled, goggled, and leathered party from the machine among the muslin gowns, smart wraps, and immaculate coverings of the conventional house party; if we but approach, they scatter in self-protection.

From these reflections it is only too plain that the automobile — like that other inartistic instrument of torture, the grand piano — is not adapted to the drawing-room. It is not quite at home in the stable; it demands a house of its own. If the friend who invites you to visit him has a machine, then accept, for he is a brother crank; but if he has none, do not fill his generous soul with dismay by running up his drive-way, sprinkling its spotless white with oil, leaving an ineradicable stain under the porte-cochère, and frightening his favorite horses into fits as you run into the stable.

But it is delightful to go through cities and out-of-the-way places, just leaving cards in a most casual manner upon people one knows. We passed through many places twice, some places three times, in careering about. Each time we called on friends; sometimes they were in, sometimes out; it was all so casual, — a cup of tea, a little chat, sometimes without shutting down the motor, — the briefest of calls, all the more charming because brief, — really, it was strange.

We see a town ahead; calling to a man by the roadside, —

"What place is that?"

"L——" is the long drawn shout as we go flying by.

"Why, the S—— s live there. I have not seen her since we were at school. I would like to stop."

"Well, just for a moment."

In a trice the machine is at the door; Mrs. S —— is out, will return in a moment; so sorry, cannot wait, leave cards; call again some other day; and we turn ten or fifteen or twenty miles to one side to see another old school-friend for five or ten minutes — just long enough for the chauffeur to oil-up while the school-mates chat.

The automobile annihilates time; it dispenses with watch and clock; it vaguely notes the coming up and the going down of the sun; but it goes right on by sunlight, by moonlight, by lamplight, by no light at all, until it is brought to a stand-still or capriciously stops of its own accord.

CHAPTER 8

The Morgan Mystery

THE OLD STONE BLACKSMITH SHOP AT STAFFORD

It was Wednesday, August 22, that we left Buffalo. In some stray notes made by my companion, I find this enthusiastic description of the start.

"Toof! toof! on it comes like a gigantic bird, its red breast throbbing, its black wings quivering; it swerves to the right, to the left, and with a quick sweep circles about and stands panting at the curb impatient to be off.

"I hastily mount and make ready for the long flight. The chauffeur grasps the iron reins, something is pulled, and something is pressed, — 'Chic—chic—whirr—whirr—r—r,' we are off. Through the rich foliage of noble trees we catch last glimpses of beautiful homes gay with flags, with masses of flowers and broad, green lawns.

"In a moment we are in the crowded streets where cars, omnibuses, cabs, carriages, trucks, and wagons of every description are hurrying pell-mell in every direction. The automobile glides like a thing of life in and out, snorting with vexation if blocked for an instant.

"Soon we are out of the hurly-burly; the homes melt away into the country; the road lengthens; we pass the old toll-gate and are fairly on our way; farewell city of jewelled towers and gay festivities.

"The day is bright, the air is sweet, and myriads of yellow butterflies flutter about us, so thickly covering the ground in places as to look like beds of yellow flowers.

"Corn-fields and pastures stretch along the roadsides; big red barns and cosey white houses seem to go skurrying by calling, 'I spy,' then vanishing in a sort of cinematographic fashion as the automobile rushes on."

As we sped onward I pointed out the places — only too well remem-bered—where the Professor had worked so hard exactly two weeks before to the day.

After luncheon, while riding about some of the less frequented streets of Batavia, we came quite unexpectedly to an old cemetery. In the corner close to the tracks of the New York Central, so placed as to be L. of C. in plain view of all persons passing on trains, is a tall, gray, weather-beaten monument, with the life-size figure of a man on the top of the square shaft. It is the monument to the memory of William Morgan who was kidnapped near that spot in the month of September, 1826, and whose fate is one of the mysteries of the last century.

To read the inscriptions I climbed the rickety fence; the grass was high, the weeds thick; the entire place showed signs of neglect and decay.

The south side of the shaft, facing the railroad, was inscribed as follows:

Sacred To The Memory Of
WILLIAM MORGAN, A NATIVE OF VIRGINIA, A CAPT. IN THE WAR OF 1812, A RESPECTABLE CITIZEN OF BATAVIA, AND A MARTYR TO THE FREEDOM OF WRITING, PRINTING, AND SPEAKING THE TRUTH. HE WAS ABDUCTED FROM NEAR THIS SPOT IN THE YEAR 1826 BY FREEMASONS, AND MURDERED FOR REVEALING THE SECRETS OF THE ORDER.

The disappearance of Morgan is still a mystery, — a myth to most people nowadays; a very stirring reality in central and western New York seventy-five years ago; even now in the localities concerned the old embers of bitter feeling show signs of life if fanned by so much as a breath.

Six miles beyond Batavia, on the road to Le Roy, is the little village of Stafford; some twenty or thirty houses bordering the highway; a church, a schoolhouse, the old stage tavern, and several buildings that are today very much as they were nearly one hundred years ago. This is the one place which remains very much as it was seventy-five years ago when Morgan was kidnapped and taken through to Canandaigua. As one approaches the little village, on the left hand side of the highway set far back in an open field is an old stone church long since abandoned and disused, but so substantially built that it has defied time and weather. It is a monument to the liberality of the people of that locality in those early days, for it was erected for the accommodation of worshippers regardless of sect; it was at the disposal of any denomination that might wish to hold services therein. Apparently the foundation of the weather-beaten structure was too liberal, for it has been many years since it has been used for any purpose whatsoever.

As one approaches the bridge crossing the little stream which cuts the village in two, there is at the left on the bank of the stream a large three-story stone dwelling. Eighty years ago the first story of this dwelling was occupied as a store; the third story was the Masonic lodge-room, and no doubt the events leading up to the disappearance of Morgan were warmly discussed within the four walls of this old building. Across from the three-story stone building is a brick house set well back from the highway, surrounded by shrubbery, and approached by a gravel walk bordered by old-fashioned boxwood hedges.

This house was built in 1812, and is still well preserved. For many years it was a quite famous private school for young ladies, kept by a Mr. Radcliffe.

Across the little bridge on the right is a low stone building now used as a blacksmith shop, but which eighty years ago was a dwelling. A little farther on the opposite side of the street is the old stage tavern, still kept as a tavern, and today in substantially the same condition inside and out as it was seventy-five years ago. It is now only a roadside inn, but before railroads were, through stages from Buffalo, Albany, and New York stopped here. A charming old lady living just opposite, said, —

"I have sat on this porch many a day and watched the stages and private coaches come rattling up with horn and whip and carrying the most famous people in the country, — all stopped there just across the road at that old red tavern; those were gay days; I shall never see the like again; but perhaps you may, for now coaches like yours stop at the old tavern almost every day."

The ballroom of the tavern remains exactly as it was, — a fireplace at one end filled with ashes of burnt-out revelries, a little railing at one side where the fiddlers sat, the old benches along the side, — all remind one of the gayeties of long ago.

In connection with the Morgan mystery the village of Stafford is interesting, because the old tavern and the three-story stone building are probably the only buildings still standing which were identified with the events leading up to the disappearance of Morgan.

The other towns, like Batavia and Canandaigua, have grown and changed, so that the old buildings have long since made way for modern. One of the last to go was the old jail at Canandaigua where Morgan was confined and from which he was taken. When that old jail was torn down some years ago, people carried away pieces of his cell as souvenirs of a mystery still fascinating because still a mystery.

As we came out of the old tavern there were a number of men gathered about the machine, looking at it. I asked them some questions about the village, and happened to say, —

"I once knew a man who, seventy-five years ago, lived in that little stone building by the bridge."

"That was in Morgan's time," said an old man, and everyone in the crowd turned instantly from the automobile to look at me.

"Yes, he lived here as a young man."

"They stopped at this very tavern with Morgan on their way through," said someone in the crowd.

"And that stone building just the other side of the bridge is where the Masons met in those days," said another.

"That's where they took Miller," interrupted the old man.

"Who was Miller?" I asked.

"He was the printer in Batavia who was getting out Morgan's book; they brought him here to Stafford, and took him up into the lodge-room in that building and tried to frighten him, but he wasn't to be frightened, so they took him on to Le Roy and let him go."

"Did they ever find out what became of Morgan?" I asked.

There was silence for a moment, and then the old man, looking first at the others, said, —

"No-o-o, not for sartain, but the people in this locality hed their opinion, and hev it yet."

"You bet they have," came from someone in the crowd.

Thursday we started for Rochester by way of Stafford and Le Roy instead of Newkirk, Byron, and Bergen, which is the more direct route and also a good road.

The morning was bright and very warm, scarcely a cloud in the sky, but there was a feeling of storm in the air, — the earth was restless.

As we neared Stafford dark clouds were gathering in the far distant skies, but not yet near enough to cause apprehension. Driving slowly into the village, we again visited the three-story stone house. Here, no doubt, as elsewhere, Morgan's forthcoming exposures were discussed and denounced, here the plot to seize him — if plot there was — may have been formed; but then there was probably no plot, conspiracy, or action on the part of any lodge or body of Masons. Morgan was in their eyes a most despicable traitor, — a man who proposed to sell — not simply disclose, but sell — the secrets of the order he joined. There is no reason to believe that he had the good of anyone at heart; that he had anything in view but his own material prosperity. He made a bargain with a printer in Batavia to expose Masonry, and lost his life in attempting to carry out that bargain. Lost his life! —who knows? The story is a strange one, as strange as anything in the Arabian Nights; there are men still living who faintly recollect the excitement, the fends and controversies which lasted for years. From Batavia to Canandaigua the name of Morgan calls forth a flood of reminiscences. A man whose father or grandfather had anything to do with the affair is a character in the community; now and then a man is found who knew a man who caught a glimpse of Morgan during that mysterious midnight ride from the Canandaigua jail over the Rochester road, and onto the end in the magazine of the old fort at Lewiston. One cannot spend twenty-four hours in this country without being drawn into the vortex of this absorbing mystery; it hangs over the entire section, lingers along the road-sides, finds outward sign and habitation in old buildings, monuments, and ruins; it echoes from the past in musty books, papers, and pamphlets; it once was politics, now is history; the years have not solved it; time is helpless.

At Le Roy we sought shelter under the friendly roof of an old, old house. How it did storm; the Rochester papers next day said that no such storm had ever been known in that part of the State. The rain fell in torrents; the main street was a stream of water emptying into the river; the flashes of lightning were followed so quickly by crashes of thunder that we knew trees and buildings were struck near by, as in fact they were. It seemed as if the heavens were laying siege to the little village and bringing to bear all nature's great guns.

The house was filled with old books and mementoes of the past; every nook and corner was interesting. In an old secretary in an upper room was found a complete history of Morgan's disappearance, together with the affidavits taken at the time and records of such court proceedings as were had. These papers had been gathered together in 1829. One by one I turned the yellow leaves and read the story from beginning to end; it is in brief as follows:

In the summer of 1826 it was rumored throughout Western New York that one William Morgan, then living in the village of Batavia, was writing an exposure of the secrets of Free Masonry, under contract with David Miller, a printer of the same place, who was to publish the pamphlet.

Morgan was a man entirely without means; he was said to have served in the War of 1812, and was known to have been a brewer, but had not made a success in business; he was rooming with a family in Batavia with his wife and two small children, one a child of two years, the other a babe of two months. He was quite irresponsible, and apparently not overscrupulous in either contracting debts or the use of the property of others.

There is not the slightest reason to believe that his so-called exposure of Masonry was prompted by any motives other than the profits he might realize from the sale of the pamphlet. Nor is there any evidence that he enjoyed the confidence of the community where he lived. His monument — as in many another case — awards him virtues he did not possess. The figure of noble bearing on the top of the shaft is the idealization of subsequent events, and probably but illy corresponds with the actual appearance of the impecunious reality. The man's fate made him a hero.

On August 9 the following notice appeared in a newspaper published in Canandaigua:

"Notice and Caution. — If a man calling himself William Morgan should intrude himself on the community, they should be on their guard, particularly the Masonic Fraternity. Morgan was in the village in May last, and his conduct while here and elsewhere calls forth this notice. Any information in relation to Morgan can be obtained by calling at the Masonic Hall in this village. Brethren and Companions are particularly requested to observe, mark, and govern themselves accordingly.

"Morgan is considered a swindler and a dangerous man.

"There are people in the village who would be happy to see this Captain Morgan.

"Canandaigua, August 9, 1826."

This notice was copied in two newspapers published in Batavia.

About the middle of August a stranger by the name of Daniel Johns appeared in Batavia and took up his lodgings in one of the public houses of the village. He made the acquaintance of Miller, offered to go in business with him, and to furnish whatever money might be necessary for the publication of the Morgan book. Miller accepted his proposition and took the man into his confidence.

As it afterwards turned out, Johns's object in seeking the partnership was to secure possession of the Morgan manuscript, so that Miller could not publish the work; the man's subsequent connection with this strange narrative appears from the affidavit of Mrs. Morgan, referred to farther on.

During the month of August, Morgan with his family boarded at a house in the heart of the village; but to avoid interruption in his work he had an upper room in the house of John David, on the other side of the creek from the town.

August 19 three well-known residents of the village accompanied by a constable from Pembroke went to David's house, inquired for David and Towsley, who both lived there with their families, and on being told they were not at home, rushed up-stairs to the room where Morgan was writing, seized him and the papers which he was even then arranging for the printer. He was taken to the county jail and kept from Saturday afternoon until Monday morning, when he was bailed out.

On the same Saturday evening the same men went to the house where Morgan boarded, and saying they had an execution, inquired of Mrs. Morgan whether her husband had any property. They were told he had none, but nevertheless two of the men went into Morgan's room and made a search for papers. On leaving the house one of them said to Mrs. Morgan, "We have just conducted your husband to jail, and shall keep him there until we find his papers."

September 8, James Ganson, who kept the tavern at Stafford, was notified from Batavia that between forty and fifty men would be there for supper. The men came and late at night departed for Batavia, where they found a number of men gathered from other points. From an affidavit taken afterwards it seems the object of the party was to destroy Miller's office, but they found Miller and Morgan had been warned. At any rate, the party dispersed without doing anything. Part of them reassembled at Ganson's, and charges of cowardice were freely exchanged; certain of the leaders were afterwards indicted for their part in this affair, but no trial was had.

To this day the business portion of Batavia stretches along both sides of a broad main street; instead of cross-streets at regular intervals there are numerous alleys leading off the main street, with here and there a wider side street.

In those days nearly all the buildings were of wood and but one or two stories in height. Miller's printing-offices occupied the second stories of two wooden buildings; a side alley separating the two buildings, dividing also, of course, the two parts of the printing establishment.

On Sunday night, September 10, fire was discovered under the stairways leading to the printing-offices; on extinguishing the blaze, straw and cotton balls saturated with turpentine were found under the stairways, and some distance from the buildings a dark lantern was found.

On this same Sunday morning, September 10, a man—the coroner of the county — in the village of Canandaigua, fifty miles east of Batavia, obtained from a justice of the peace a warrant for the arrest of Morgan on the charge of stealing a shirt and a cravat in the month of May from an innkeeper named Kingsley.

Having obtained the warrant, which was directed to him as coroner, the complainant called a constable, and together with four well-known residents of Canandaigua they hired a special stage and started for Batavia.

At Avon, Caledonia, and Le Roy they were joined by others who seemed to understand that Morgan was to be arrested.

At Stafford they stopped for supper at Ganson's tavern. After supper they proceeded towards Batavia, but stopped about a mile and a half east of the village, certain of the party returning with the stage.

Early the next morning Morgan was arrested, and an extra stage engaged to take the party back. The driver, becoming uneasy as to the regularity of the proceedings, at first refused to start, but was persuaded to go as far as Stafford, where Ganson — whom the driver knew — said everything was all right and that he would assume all responsibility.

About sunset of the same day—Monday, September 11—they arrived at Canandaigua, and Morgan was at once examined by the justice; the evidence was held insufficient and the prisoner discharged.

The same complainant immediately produced a claim for two dollars which had been assigned to him. Morgan admitted the debt, confessed judgment, and pulled off his coat, offering it as security.

The constable refused to take the coat and took Morgan to jail.

Tuesday noon, September 12, a crowd of strangers appeared in Batavia, assembling at Donald's tavern. A constable went to Miller's office, arrested him, and took him to the tavern, where he was detained in a room for about two hours. He was then put in an open wagon with some men, all strangers to him. The constable mounted his horse and the party proceeded to Stafford. Arriving there Miller was conducted to the third story of the stone building beside the creek, and was there confined, guarded by five men.

About dusk the constable and the crowd took Miller to Le Roy, where he was taken before the justice who had issued the warrant, when all his prosecutors, together with constable and warrant, disappeared. As no one appeared against the prisoner, the justice told him he was at liberty to go.

From the docket of the justice it appeared that the warrant had been issued at the request of Daniel Johns, Miller's partner.

The leaders were indicted for riot, assault, and false imprisonment, tried, three found guilty and imprisoned. At the trial there was evidence to show that on the morning of the 12th a meeting was held in the third story of the stone building at Stafford, a leader selected, and plans arranged.

On the evening of Tuesday 12th a neighbor of Morgan's called at the Canandaigua jail and asked to see Morgan The jailer was absent. His wife permitted the man to speak to Morgan, and the man said that he had come to pay the debt for which Morgan was committed and to take him home. Morgan was asked if he were willing to go; he answered that he was willing, but that it did not matter particularly that night, for he could just as well wait until morning; but the man said "No," that he would rather take him out that night, for he had run around all day for him and was very tired and wished to get home. The man offered to deposit with the jailer's wife five dollars as security for the payment of the debt and all costs, but she would not let Morgan out, saying that she did not know the man and that he was not the owner of the judgment.

The man went out and was gone a few minutes, and brought back a well-known resident of the village of Canandaigua and the owner of the judgment; these two men said that it was all right for the jailer's wife to accept two dollars, the amount of the judgment, and release Morgan. Taking the money, the woman opened the inside door of the prison, and Morgan was requested to get ready quickly and come out. He was soon ready, and walked out of the front door between the man who had called for him and another. The jailer's wife while fastening the inside prison-door heard a cry of murder near the outer door of the jail, and running to the door she saw Morgan struggling with the two men who had come for him. He continued to scream and cry in the most distressing manner, at the same time struggling with all his strength; his voice was suppressed by something that was put over his mouth, and a man following behind rapped loudly upon the well-curb with a stick; a carriage came up, Morgan was put in it by the two men with him, and the carriage drove off. It was a moonlight night, and the jailer's wife clearly saw all that transpired, and even remembered that the horses were gray. Neither the man who made the complaint, nor the resident of Canandaigua who came to the jail and advised the jailer's wife that she could safely let Morgan go, went with the carriage. They picked up Morgan's hat, which was lost in the struggle, and watched the carriage drive away.

The account given by the wife of the jailer was corroborated by a number of entirely reliable and reputable witnesses.

A man living near the jail went to the door of his house and saw the men struggling in the street, one of them apparently down and making noises of distress; the man went towards the struggling man, and asked a man who was a little behind the others what was the matter, to which he answered, "Nothing; only a man has been let out of jail, and been taken on a warrant, and is going to be tried, or have his trial."

In January following, when the feeling was growing against the abductors of Morgan, the three men in Canandaigua most prominently connected with all that transpired at the jail on the night in question made statements in court under oath, which admitted the facts to be substantially as above outlined, except they insisted that they did not know why Morgan struggled before getting into the carriage. These men expressed regret that they did not go to the assistance of Morgan, and insisted that was the only fault they committed on the night in question. They admitted that they understood that Morgan was compiling a book on the subject of Masonry at the instigation of Miller the publisher at Batavia, and alleged that he was getting up the book solely for pecuniary profit, and they believed it was desirable to remove Morgan to some place beyond the influence of Miller, where his friends and acquaintances might convince him of the impropriety of his conduct and persuade him to abandon the publication of the book.

In passing sentence, the court said:

"The legislature have not seen fit, perhaps, from the supposed improbability that the crime would be attempted, to make your offence a felony. Its grade and punishment have been left to the provisions of the common law, which treats it as a misdemeanor, and punishes it with fine and imprisonment in the common jail. The court are of opinion that your liberty ought to be made to answer for the liberty of Morgan: his person was restrained by force; and the court, in the exercise of its lawful powers, ought not to be more tender of your liberty than you, in the plenitude of lawless force, were of his."

It is quite clear that up to this time none of the to-do parties connected directly or indirectly with the abduction of Morgan had any intention whatsoever of doing him bodily harm. If such had been their purpose, the course they followed was foolish in the extreme. The simple fact was the Masons were greatly excited over the threatened exposure of the secrets of their order by one of their own members, and they desired to get hold of the manuscript and proofs and prevent the publication, and the misguided hot-heads who were active in the matter thought that by getting Morgan away from Miller they could persuade him to abandon his project. This theory is borne out by the fact that on the day Morgan was taken to Canandaigua several prominent men of Batavia called upon Mrs. Morgan and told her that if she would give up to the Masons the papers she had in her possession Morgan would be brought back. She gave up all the papers she could find; they were submitted to Johns, the former partner of Miller, who said that part of the manuscript was not there. However, the men took Mrs. Morgan to Canandaigua, stopping at Avon over night. These men expected to find Morgan still in Canandaigua, but were surprised to learn that he had been taken away the night before, whereupon Mrs. Morgan, having left her two small children at home, returned as quickly as possible.

So far as Morgan's manuscript is concerned, it seems that a portion of it was already in the hands of Miller, and another portion secreted inside of a bed at the time he was arrested, so that not long after his disappearance what purports to be his book was published.

Nearly two years later, in August, 1828, three men were tried for conspiracy to kidnap and carry away Morgan. At that time it was believed by many that Morgan was either simply detained abroad or in hiding, although it was strenuously insisted by others that he had been killed. All that was ever known of his movements after he left the jail at Canandaigua on the night of September 11 was developed in the testimony taken at this trial.

One witness who saw the carriage drive past the jail testified that a man was put in by four others, who got in after him and the carriage drove away; the witness was near the men when they got into the carriage, and as it turned west he heard one of them cry to the driver, "Why don't you drive faster? why don't you drive faster?"

The driver testified that some time prior to the date in question a man came to him and arranged for him to take a party to Rochester on or about the 12th. On the night in question he took his yellow carriage and gray horses about nine o'clock and drove just beyond the Canandaigua jail on the Palmyra road. A party of five got into the carriage, but he heard no noise and saw no resistance, nor did he know any of the men. He was told to go on beyond Rochester, and he took the Lewiston road. On arriving at Hanford's one of the party got out; he then drove about one hundred yards beyond the house, stopping near a piece of woods, where the others who were in the carriage got out, and he turned around and drove back.

Another man who lived at Lewiston and worked as a stage-driver said that he was called between ten and twelve o'clock at night and told to drive a certain carriage into a back street alongside of another carriage which he found standing there without any horse attached to it; some men were standing near it. He drove alongside the carriage, and one or two men got out of it and got into his hack. He saw no violence, but on stopping at a point about six miles farther on some of the men got out, and while they were conversing, someone in the carriage asked for water in a whining voice, to which one of the men replied, "You shall have some in a moment." No water was handed to the person in the carriage, but the men got in, and he drove them onto a point about half a mile from Fort Niagara, where they told him to stop; there were no houses there; the party, four in number, got out and proceeded side by side towards the fort; he drove back with his carriage.

A man living in Lewiston swore that he went to his door and saw a carriage coming, which went a little distance farther on, stopping beside another carriage which was in the street without horses; he recognized the driver of the carriage and one other man; he thought something strange was going on and went into his garden, where he had a good view of what took place in the road; he saw a man go from the box of the carriage, which had driven by, to the one standing in the street and open the door; someone got out backward with the assistance of two men in the carriage. The person who was taken out had no hat, but a handkerchief on his head, and appeared to be intoxicated and helpless. They took him to the other carriage and all got in. One of the men went back and took something from the carriage they had left, which seemed to be a jug, and then they drove off.

At the trial in question, the testimony of a man by the name of Giddins, who had the custody of old Fort Niagara, was not received because it appeared he had no religious beliefs whatsoever, but his brother-in-law testified that on a certain night in September, shortly after the events narrated, he was staying at Giddins's house, Which was twenty or thirty rods from the magazine of the old fort; that before going to the installation of the lodge at Lewiston he went with Giddins to the magazine. Previously to starting out Giddins had a pistol, which he requested the witness to carry, but witness declined. Giddins had something else with him, which the witness did not recognize. When they came within about two rods of the magazine, Giddins went up to the door and something was said inside the door. A man's voice came from inside the magazine; witness was alarmed, and thought he had better get out of the way, and he at once retreated, followed soon after by Giddins.

From the old records it seemed that the evidence tracing Morgan to the magazine of old Fort Niagara was satisfactory to court and jury; but what became of him no man knows. In January, 1827, the fort and magazine were visited by certain committees appointed to make investigations, who reported in detail the condition of the magazine, which seemed to indicate that someone had been confined therein not long before, and that the prisoner had made violent and reiterated efforts to force his way out. A good many hearsay statements were taken to the effect that Morgan was as a matter of fact put in the magazine and kept there some days.

Governor De Witt Clinton issued three proclamations, two soon after September, 1826, and the last dated March 19, 1827, offering rewards for "Authentic information of the place where the said William Morgan has been conveyed," and "for the discovery of the said William Morgan, if alive; and, if murdered, a reward of two thousand dollars for the discovery of the offender or offenders, etc."

In the autumn of 1827 a body was cast up on the shore of Lake Ontario near the mouth of Oak Orchard Creek. Mrs. Morgan and a Dr. Strong identified the body as that of William Morgan by a scar on the foot and by the teeth.

The identification was disputed; the disappearance of Morgan was then a matter of politics, and the anti-masons, headed by Thurlow Weed, originated the saying, "It's a good enough Morgan for us until you produce the live one," which afterwards become current political slang in the form, "It's a good enough Morgan until after election."

CHAPTER 9

Through Western New York

IN THE MUD

The afternoon was drawing to a close, the rain had partially subsided, but the trees were heavy with water, and the streets ran rivulets.

Prudence would seem to dictate remaining in Le Roy over-night, but, so far as roads are concerned, it is always better to start out in, or immediately after, a rain than to wait until the water has soaked in and made the mud deep. A heavy rain washes the surface off the roads; it is better not to give it time to penetrate; we therefore determined to start at once.

There was not a soul on the streets as we pulled out a few moments after five o'clock, and in the entire ride of some thirty miles we met scarcely more than three or four teams.

We took the road by Bergen rather than through Caledonia; both roads are good, but in very wet weather the road from Bergen to Rochester is apt to be better than that from Caledonia, as it is more sandy.

To Bergen, eight miles, we found hard gravel, with one steep hill to descend; from Bergen in, it was sandy, and after the rain, was six inches deep in places with soft mud.

It was slow progress and eight o'clock when we pulled into Rochester.

We were given rooms where all the noises of street and trolley could be heard to best advantage; sleep was a struggle, rest an impossibility.

Hotel construction has quite kept pace with the times, but hotel location is a tradition of the dark ages, when to catch patrons it was necessary to get in their way.

At Syracuse the New York Central passes through the principal hotels, —the main tracks bisecting the dining-rooms, with side tracks down each corridor and a switch in each bed-room; but this is an extreme instance.

It was well enough in olden times to open taverns on the highways; an occasional coach would furnish the novelty and break the monotony, but people could sleep.

The erection of hotels in close proximity to railroad tracks, or upon the main thoroughfares of cities where stone or asphalt pavements resound to every hoof-fall, and where street cars go whirring and clanging by all night long, is something more than an anachronism; it is a fiendish disregard of human comfort.

Paradoxical as it may seem, — a pious but garrulous old gentleman was one time invited to lead in prayer; consenting, he approached the throne of grace with becoming humility, saying, "Paradoxical as it may seem, O Lord, it is nevertheless true," etc., the phrase is a good one, it lingers in the ear, — therefore, once more, — paradoxical as it may seem, it is nevertheless true that those who go about all day in machines do not like to be disturbed by machines at night.

We soon learned to keep away from the cities at night. It is so much more delightful to stop in smaller towns and villages; your host is glad to see you; you are quite the guest of honor perhaps the only guest; there is a place in the adjoining stable for the machine; the men are interested, and only too glad to care for it and help in the morning; the best the house affords is offered; as a rule the rooms are quite good, the beds clean, and nowadays many of these small hotels have rooms with baths; the table is plain; but while automobiling one soon comes to prefer plain country living.

In the larger cities it costs a fortune in tips before the machine and oneself are well housed; to enter Albany, Boston, or New York at night, find your hotel, find the automobile station, find your luggage, and find yourself, is a bore.

No one who has ever ridden day after day in the country cares anything about riding in cities; it is as artificial and monotonous as riding a hunter over pavements. If one could just approach a city at night, steal into it, enjoy its lights and shadows, its confusion and strange sounds, all in passing, and slip through without stopping long enough to feel the thrust of the reality, it would be delightful. But the charm disappears, the dream is brought to earth, the vision becomes tinsel when you draw up in front of a big caravansary and a platoon of uniformed porters, bell-boys, and pages swoop down upon everything you have, including your pocketbook; then the Olympian clerk looks at you doubtfully, puzzled for the first time in his life, does not know whether you are a mill-hand from Pittsburg who should be assigned a hall bed-room in the annex, or a millionaire from Newport who should be tendered the entire establishment on a silver platter.

The direct road from Rochester to Syracuse is by way of Pittsford, Palmyra, Newark, Lyons, Clyde, Port Byron, and Camillus, but it is neither
so good nor so interesting as the old roads through Geneva and Auburn.

In going from Buffalo to Albany *via* Syracuse, Rochester is to the north
and some miles out of the way; unless one especially desires to visit the
city, it is better to leave it to one side.

Genesee Street out of Buffalo is Genesee Street into Syracuse and Utica;
it is the old highway between Buffalo and Albany, and may be followed
today from end to end.

Instead of turning to the northeast at Batavia and going through
Newkirk, Byron, Bergen, North Chili, and Gates to Rochester, keep more
directly east through Le Roy, Caledonia, Avon, and Canandaigua to
Geneva; the towns are old, the hotels, most of them, good, the roads are
generally gravel and the country interesting; it is old New York. No one
driving through the State for pleasure would think of taking the direct
road from Rochester to Syracuse; the beautiful portions of this western
end of the State are to the south, in the Genesee and Wyoming Valleys,
and through the lake region.

We left Rochester at ten o'clock, Saturday, the 24th, intending to go east
by Egypt, Macedon, Palmyra, — the Oriental route, as my Companion
called it; but after leaving Pittsford we missed the road and lost ourselves
among the hills, finding several grades so steep and soft that we both were
obliged to dismount.

An old resident was decidedly of the opinion that the roads to the
southeast were better than those to the northeast, and we turned from the
Nile route towards Canandaigua.

Though the roads were decidedly better, in many places being well
gravelled, the heavy rains of the previous two days made the going slow,
and it was one-thirty before we pulled up at the old hotel in Canandaigua
for dinner.

As the machine had been there before, we were greeted as friends. The
old negro porter is a character, — quite the irresponsible head of the entire
establishment.

Sambo carried our things in, talking all the time.

"Now you jes' go right into dinnah; I'll take keer of the auto'bile; I'll
see that nun of those ign'rant folk stannin' roun' lay their han's on it; they
think Sambo doan know an auto'bile; didn't I see you heah befoh? an'
didn't I hole de hose when you put de watah in? Me an' you are de only

two pussons in dis whole town who knows about de auto'bile, — jes' me an' you."

After dinner we rode down the broad main street and around the lake to the left in going to Geneva. Barring the fact that the roads were soft in places, the afternoon's ride was delightful, the roads being generally very good.

It was about five o'clock when we came to the top of the hills overlooking Geneva and the silvery lake beyond. It was a sight not to be forgotten by the American traveller, for this country has few towns so happily situated as the village of Geneva, — a cluster of houses against a wooded slope with the lake like a mirror below.

The little hotel was almost new and very good; the rooms were large and comfortable. There was but one objection, and that the location at the very corner of the busiest and noisiest streets. But Geneva goes to bed early, — even on Saturday nights, — and by ten or eleven o'clock the streets were quiet, while on Sunday mornings there is nothing to disturb one before the bells ring for church.

We were quite content to rest this first Sunday out.

It was so delightfully quiet all the morning that we lounged about and read until dinner-time. In the afternoon a walk, and in the evening friends came to supper with us. In a moment of ambitious emulation of metropolitan customs the small hotel had established a roof garden, with music two or three evenings a week, but the innovation had not proven profitable; the roof remained with some iron framework that once supported awnings, several disconsolate tables, and some lonesome iron chairs; we visited this scene of departed glory and obtained a view of the lake at evening.

The irregular outlines of the long shadows of the hills stretched far out over the still water; beyond these broken lines the slanting rays of the setting sun fell upon the surface of the lake, making it to shine like a mass of burnished silver.

Some white sails glimmered in the light far across; near by we caught the sound of church-bells; the twilight deepened, the shadows lengthened, the luminous stretch of water grew narrower and narrower until it disappeared entirely and all was dark upon the lake, save here and there the twinkle of lights from moving boats, — shifting stars in the void of night.

The morning was bright as we left Geneva, but the roads, until we struck the State road, were rough and still muddy from the recent rains.

It was but a short run to Auburn, and from there into Syracuse the road is a fine gravel.

The machine had developed a slight pounding and the rear-axle showed signs of again parting at the differential.

After luncheon the machine was run into a machine shop, and three hours were spent in taking up the lost motion in the eccentric strap, at the crank-pin, and in a loose bushing.

On opening up the differential gear case both set-screws holding the axles were found loose. The factory had been most emphatically requested to put in larger keys so as to fit the key-ways snugly and to lock these set-screws in some way — neither of these things had been done; and both halves of the rear-axle were on the verge of working out.

Small holes were bored through the set-screws, wires passed through and around the shoulders of the gears, and we had no further trouble from this source.

It was half-past five before we left Syracuse for Oneida. The road is good, and the run of twenty-seven miles was made in little over two hours, arriving at the small, old-fashioned tavern in Oneida at exactly seven forty-five.

A number of old-timers dropped into the hotel office that evening to see what was going on and hear about the strange machine. Great stories were exchanged on all sides; the glories of Oneida quite eclipsed the lesser claims of the automobile to fame and notoriety, for it seemed that some of the best-known men of New York and Chicago were born in the village or the immediate vicinity; the landmarks remain, traditions are intact, the men departed to seek their fortunes elsewhere, but their successes are the town's fame.

The genial proprietor of the hotel carried his seventy-odd years and two hundred and sixty pounds quite handily in his shirt-sleeves, moving with commendable celerity from office to barroom, supplying us in the front room with information and those in the back with refreshment.

"So you never heard that those big men were born in this locality. That's strange; tho't ev'rybody knew that. Why 'Neida has produced more famous men than any town same size in 'Merika, — Russell Sage, General New, — comin'" (to those in the barroom); "say, you fellers, can't you wait?"

As he disappeared in the rear we heard his rotund voice, "What'll you take? Was jest tellin' that chap with the threshin'-machine a thing or two about this country. Rye? no, thet's Bourbon — the reel corn juice — ten years in wood."

"Mixed across the street at the drugstore — ha! ha! ha!" interrupted someone.

"Don't be faceshus, Sam; this ain't no sody-fountin."

"Where'd that feller cum frum with his steam pianer, — Syr'cuse?"

"Naw! Chicago."

"Great cranberries! you don't say so, — all the way from Chicago! When did he start?"

"Day 'fore yesterday," replied the old man, and we could hear him putting back the bottles; a chorus of voices, —

"What!"

"Holy Mo — "

"Day afore yester — say, look here, you're jokin'."

"Mebbe I am, but if you don't believe it, ask him."

"Why Chicago is further'n Buf'lo — an' that's faster'n a train."

"Yes," drawled the old man; "he passed the Empire Express th' other side Syr'cuse."

"Get out."

"What do you take us fer?"

"Wall, when you cum in, I took you fer fellers who knowed the diff'rence betwixt whiskey and benzine, but I see my mistake. You fellers shud buy your alc'hol across the way at the drugstore; it don't cost s'much, and burns better."

"Thet's one on us. Your whiskey is all right, grandpa, the reel corn juice — ten year in wood — too long in bottl'spile if left over night, so pull the stopper once more."

CHAPTER 10

The Mohawk Valley

IN THE VALLEY

On looking over the machine the next morning, Tuesday, the 27th, the large cap-screws holding the bearings of the main-shaft were found slightly loose. The wrench with the machine was altogether too light to turn these screws up as tight as they should be; it was therefore necessary to have a wrench made from tool steel; that required about half an hour, but it was time well spent.

The road from Oneida to Utica is very good; rolling but no steep grades; some sand, but not deep; some clay, but not rough; for the most part gravel.

The run of twenty miles was quickly made. We stopped only for a moment to inquire for letters and then on to Herkimer by the road on the north side of the valley. Returning some weeks later we came by the south road, through Frankford, between the canal and the railroad tracks, through Mohawk and Ilion. This is the better known and the main travelled road; but it is far inferior to the road on the north; there are more hills on the latter, some of the grades being fairly steep, but in dry weather the north road is more picturesque and more delightful in every way, while in wet weather there is less deep mud.

At Herkimer, eighteen and one-half miles from Utica and thirty-eight from Oneida, we had luncheon, then inquired for gasoline. Most astonishing! in the entire village no gasoline to be had. A town of most respectable size, hotel quite up to date, large brick blocks of stores, enterprise apparent — but no gasoline. Only one man handled it regularly, an old man who drove about the country with his tank-wagon distributing kerosene and gasoline; he had no place of business but his house, and he happened to be entirely out of gasoline. In two weeks the endurance run of the Automobile Club of America would be through there; at Herkimer those in the contest were to stop for the night, — and no gasoline.

In the entire pilgrimage of over two thousand miles through nine States and the province of Ontario, we did not find a town or village of any size where gasoline could not be obtained, and frequently we found it at cross-road stores, — but not at Herkimer.

Happily there was sufficient gasoline in the tank to carry us on; besides, we always had a gallon in reserve. At the next village we found all we needed.

When we returned through Herkimer some weeks later nearly every store had gasoline.

If hotels, stables, and drugstores, wherever automobiles are apt to come, would keep a five-gallon can of gasoline on hand, time and trouble would be saved, and drivers of automobiles would be only too glad to pay an extra price for the convenience.

The grades of gasoline sold in this country vary from the common so-called "stove gasoline," or sixty-eight, to seventy-four. The country dealers are becoming wise in their generation, and all now insist they keep only seventy-four. As a matter of fact nearly all that is sold in both cities and country is the "stove gasoline," because it is kept on hand principally for stoves and torches, and they do not require higher than sixty-eight. In fact, one is fortunate if the gasoline tests so high as that.

American machines, as a rule, get along very well with the low grades, but many of the foreign machines require the better grades. If a machine will not use commercial stove gasoline, the only safe thing is to carry a supply of higher grade along, and that is a nuisance.

It is difficult to find a genuine seventy-four even in the cities, since it is commonly sold only in barrels. If the exhaust of a gasoline stationary engine is heard anywhere along the road-side, stop, for there will generally be found a barrel or two of the high-grade, and a supply may be laid in.

The best plan, however, is to have a carburetor and motor that will use the ordinary "stove-grade;" as a matter of fact, it contains more carbon and more explosive energy if thoroughly ignited, but it does not make gas so readily in cold weather and requires a good hot spark.

All day we rode on through the valley, now far up on the hill-sides, now down by the meadows; past Palatine Church, Palatine Bridge; through Fonda and Amsterdam to Schenectady.

It was a glorious ride. The road winds along the side of the valley, following the graceful curves and swellings of the hills. The little towns are so lost in the recesses that one comes upon them quite unexpectedly, and, whirling through their one long main street, catches glimpses of quaint churches and buildings which fairly overhang the highway, and narrow vistas of lawns, trees, shrubbery, and flowers; then all is hidden by the next bend in the road.

During the long summer afternoon we sped onward through this beautiful valley. Far down on the tracks below trains would go scurrying by; now and then a slow freight would challenge our competition; train-men would look up curiously; occasionally an engineer would sound a note of defiance or a blast of victory with his whistle.

The distant river followed lazily along, winding hither and thither through the lowland, now skirting the base of the hills, now bending far to the other side as if resentful of such rude obstructions to its once impetuous will.

Far across on the distant slopes we could see the cattle grazing, and farther still tiny specks that were human beings like ourselves moving upon the landscape. Nature's slightest effort dwarfs man's mightiest achievements. That great railroad with its many tracks and rushing trains seemed a child's plaything, —a noisy, whirring, mechanical toy beside the lazy river; for did not that placid, murmuring, meandering stream in days gone by hollow out this valley? did not nature in moments of play rear those hills and carve out those distant mountains? Compared with these traces of giant handiwork, what are the works of man? just little putterings for our own convenience, just little utilizations of waste energies for our own purposes.

One should view nature with the setting sun. It may gratify a bustling curiosity to see nature at her toilet, but that is the part of a "Peeping Tom."

The hour of sunrise is the hour for work, it is the hour when every living thing feels the impulse to do something. The birds do not fly to the tree-tops to view the morning sun, the animals do not rush forth from their lairs to watch the landscape lighten with the morning's glow; no, all nature is refreshed and eager to be doing, not seeing; acting, not thinking. Man is no exception to this all-embracing rule; his innate being protests against idleness; the most secret cells of his organization are charged to overflowing with energy and demand relief in work.

Morning is not the hour for contemplation; but when evening comes, as the sun sinks towards the west, and lengthening shadows make it seem as if all nature were stretching herself in repose, then do we love to rest and contemplate the rich loveliness of the earth and the infinite tenderness of the heavens. Every harsh line, every glare of light, every crude tone has disappeared. We stroke nature and she purrs. We sink at our ease in a bed of moss and nature nestles at our side; we linger beside the silvery brook and it sings to us; we listen attentively to the murmuring trees and they whisper to us; we gaze upon the frowning hills and they smile upon us. And by and by as the shadows deepen all outlines are lost, and we see vaguely the great masses of tone and color; nature becomes heroic; the petty is dissolved; the insignificant is lost; hills and trees and streams are blended in one mighty composition, in the presence of which all but the impalpable soul of man is as nothing.

We left Schenectady at nine o'clock, taking the Troy road as far as Latham's Corners, then to the right into Albany.

We reached the city at half-past ten. Albany is not a convenient place for automobiles. There are no special stations for the storing of machines, and the stables are most inaccessible on account of the hills and steep approaches.

CHAPTER 11

The Valley of Lebanon

THE SICK TURKEY

It was four o'clock, next day, when we left Albany, going down Green Street and crossing the long bridge, taking the straight road over the ridges for Pittsfield.

Immediately on leaving the eastern end of the bridge the ascent of a long steep grade is begun. This is the first ridge, and from this on for fifteen miles is a succession of ridges, steep rocky hills, and precipitous declines. These continue until Brainerd is reached, where the valley of Lebanon begins.

These ridges can be partially avoided by turning down the Hudson to the right after crossing the bridge and making a detour to Brainerd; the road is about five miles longer, but is very commonly taken by farmers going to the city with heavy loads, and may well be taken by all who wish to avoid a series of stiff grades.

Many farmers were amazed to hear we had come over the hills instead of going around, and wondered how the machine managed to do it.

Popular notions concerning the capabilities of a machine are interesting; people estimate its strength and resources by those of a horse. In speaking of roads, farmers seem to assume the machine — like the horse — will not mind one or two hills, no matter how steep, but that it will mind a series of grades, even though none are very stiff.

Steam and electric automobiles do tire, — that is, long pulls through heavy roads or up grades tell on them, — the former has trouble in keeping up steam, the latter rapidly consumes its store of electricity. The gasoline machine does not tire. Within its limitations it can keep going indefinitely, and it is immaterial whether it is up or down grade — save in the time made; it will go all day through deep mud, or up steep hills, quite as smoothly, though by no means so fast, as on the level; but let it come to one hole, spot, or hill that is just beyond the limit of its power, and it is stuck; it has no reserve force to draw upon. The steam machine can stop a moment, accumulate two or three hundred pounds of steam, open the throttle and, for a few moments, exert twice its normal energy to get out of the difficulty.

It is not a series of hills that deters the gasoline operator, but the one hill, the one grade, the one bad place, which is just beyond the power he has available. The road the farmer calls good may have that one bad place or hill in it, and must therefore be avoided. The road that is pronounced bad may be, every foot of it, well within the power of the machine, and is therefore the road to take.

In actual road work the term "horsepower" is very misleading.

When steam-engines in early days began to take the place of horses, they were rated as so many horsepower according to the number of horses they displaced. It then became important to find out what was the power of the horse. Observing the strong dray horses used by the London breweries, Watt found that a horse could go two and one-half miles per hour and at the same time raise a weight of one hundred and fifty pounds suspended by a rope over a pulley; this is equivalent to thirty-three thousand pounds raised one foot in one minute, which is said to be one horsepower.

No horse, of course, could raise thirty-three thousand pounds a foot or any portion of a foot in a minute or an hour, but the horse can travel at the rate of two and one-half miles an hour raising a weight of one hundred and fifty pounds, and the horse can do more; while it cannot move so heavy a weight as thirty-three thousand pounds, it can in an emergency and by sudden strain move much more than one hundred and fifty pounds; with good foothold it can pull more than its own weight along a road, out of a hole, or up a hill. It could not lift or pull so great a weight very far; in fact, no farther than the equivalent of approximately thirty-three thousand pounds raised one foot in one minute; but for the few seconds necessary a very great amount of energy is at the command of the driver of the horse. Hence eight horses, or even four, or two can do things on the road that an eight horsepower gasoline machine cannot do; for the gasoline machine cannot concentrate all its power into the exertion of a few moments. If it is capable of lifting a given load up a given grade at a certain speed on its lowest gear, it cannot lift twice the load up the same grade, or the same load up a steeper grade in double the time, for its resources are exhausted when the limit of the power developed through the lowest gear is reached. The grade may be only a mud hole, out of which the rear wheels have to rise only two feet to be free, but it is as fatal to progress as a hill a mile long.

Of course it is always possible to race the engine, throw in the clutch, and gain some power from the momentum of the fly-wheel, and many a bad place may be surmounted step by step in this way; but this process has its limitations also, and the fact remains that with a gasoline machine it is possible to carry a given load only so fast, but if the machine moves it all, it will continue to move on until the load is increased, or the road changes for the worse.

When the farmer hears of an eight horsepower machine he thinks of the wonderful things eight good horses can do on the road, and is surprised when the machine fails to go up hills that teams travel every day; he does not understand it, and wonders where the power comes in. He is not enough of a mechanic to reflect that the eight horsepower is demonstrated in the carrying of a ton over average roads one hundred and fifty miles in ten hours, something eight horses could not possibly do.

Just as we were entering the valley of Lebanon, beyond the village of Brainerd, while going down a slight descent, my Companion exclaimed: "The wheel is coming off." I threw out the clutch, applied the brake, looked, and saw the left front wheel roll gracefully and quite deliberately out from under the big metal mud guard; the carriage settled down at that corner, and the end of the axle ploughed a furrow in the road for a few feet, when we came to a stop.

The steering-head had broken short off at the inside of the hub. We were not going very fast at the time, and the heavy metal mud guard which caught the wheel, acting as a huge brake, saved us from a bad smash.

On examination, the shank of the steering-head was found to contain two large flaws, which reduced its strength more than one-half, and the surprising thing was that it had not parted long before, when subjected to much severer strains.

This was a break that no man could repair on the road. Under pressure of circumstances the steering-head could have been taken to the nearest blacksmith shop and a weld made, but that would require time, and the results would be more than doubtful. By far the easier thing to do was to wire the factory for a new head and patiently wait its coming.

Happily, we landed in the hands of a retired farmer, whose generous hospitality embraced our tired selves as well as the machine.

Before supper a telegram was sent from Brainerd to the factory for a new steering-head. While waiting inside for the operator to finish selling tickets for the one evening train about to arrive, a curious crowd gathered outside about my host, and the questions asked were plainly audible; the names are fictitious.

"What'r ye down t' the stashun fur this hur o' day, Joe?"

"Broke my new aut'mobile," carelessly replied my host, flicking a fly off the nigh side of his horse.

"Shu!"

"What'r given us?"

"Git out—"

"You ain't got no aut'mobile," chorused the crowd.

"Mebbe I haven't; but if you fellows know an aut'mobile from a hay rake, you might take a look in my big barn an' let me know what you see."

"Say, Joe, you're jokin',—hev you really got one?"

"You can look for yourselves."

"I saw one go through here 'bout six o'clock," interrupted a new-comer. "Great Jehosephat, but 't went like a streak of greased lightnin'."

"War that your'n, Joe?"

"Well—"

"Naw," said the new-comer, scornfully. "Joe ain't got no aut'mobile; there's the feller in there now who runs it," and the crowd turned my way with such interest that I turned to the little table and wrote the despatch, quite losing the connection of the subdued murmurs outside; but it was quite evident from the broken exclamations that my host was filling the populace up with information interesting inversely to its accuracy.

"Mile a minute—faster'n a train—Holy Moses! what's that, Joe? broke axle—telegraphed—how many—four more—you don't say so?—what's his name? I'll bet it's Vanderbilt. Don't you believe it—it costs money to run one of those machines. I'll bet he's a dandy from way back—stopping at your house—bridal chamber—that's right—you want to kill the fatted calf for them fellers—say—"

But further comments were cut short as I came out, jumped in, and we drove back to a good supper by candle-light.

The stars were shining over head, the air was clear and crisp, down in the valley of Lebanon the mist was falling, and it was cool that night. Lulled by the monotonous song of the tree-toad and the deep bass croaking of frogs by the distant stream, we fell asleep.

There was nothing to do next day. The new steering-head could not possibly arrive until the morning following. As the farm was worked by a tenant, our host had little to do, and proposed that we drive to the Shaker village a few miles beyond.

The visit is well worth making, and we should have missed it entirely if the automobile had not broken down, for the new State road over the mountain does not go through the village, but back of it.

From the new road one can look down upon the cluster of large buildings on the side of the mountain, but the old roads are so very steep, with such interesting names as "Devil's Elbow," and the like, that they would not tempt an automobile. Many with horses get out and walk at the worst places.

One wide street leads through the settlement; on each side are the huge community buildings, seven in all, each occupied by a "family," so called, or community, and each quite independent in its management and enterprises from the others; the common ties being the meeting-house near the centre and the school-house a little farther on.

We stopped at the North Family simply because it was the first at hand, and we were hungry. Ushered into a little reception-room in one of the outer buildings, we were obliged to wait for dinner until the party preceding us had finished, for the little dining-room devoted to strangers had only one table, seating but six or eight, and it seemed to be the commendable policy of the institution to serve each party separately.

A printed notice warned us that dinner served after one o'clock cost ten cents per cover extra, making the extravagant charge of sixty cents. We arrived just in time to be entitled to the regular rate, but the dilatory tactics of the party in possession kept us beyond the hour and involved us in the extra expense, with no compensation in the shape of extra dishes. Morally and — having tendered ourselves within the limit — legally we were entitled to dine at the regular rate, or the party ahead should have paid the additional tariff, but the good sister could not see the matter in that light, plead ignorance of law, and relied entirely upon custom.

The man who picks up a Shaker maiden for a fool will let her drop.

Having waited until nearly famished, the sister blandly told us, as if it were a matter of local interest, but otherwise of small consequence, that the North Family were strict vegetarians, serving no meat whatsoever; the the only meat family was at the other end of the village.

We were ready for meat, for chickens, ducks, green goose, anything that walked on legs; we were not ready for pumpkin, squash, boiled potatoes, canned peas, and cabbage; but a theory as well as a condition confronted us; it was give in or move on. We gave in, but for fifteen cents more per plate bargained for preserves, maple syrup, and honey, — for something cloying to deceive the outraged palate.

But that dinner was a revelation of what a good cook can do with vegetables in season; it was the quintessence of delicacy, the refinement of finesse, the veritable apotheosis of the kitchen garden; meat would have been brutal, the intrusion of a chop inexcusable, the assertion of a steak barbarous, even a terrapin would have felt quite out of place amidst things so fragrant and impalpable as the marvellous preparations of vegetables from that wonderful Shaker kitchen.

Everything was good, but the various concoctions of sweet corn were better; and such sweet corn! it is still a savory recollection.

Then the variety of preserves, jellies, and syrups; fifteen cents extra were never bestowed to better advantage. We cast our coppers upon the water and they returned Spanish galleons laden with good things to eat.

After dining, we were walked through the various buildings, up stairs and down, through kitchens, pantries, and cellars, — a wise exercise after so bountiful a repast. In the cellar we drank something from a bottle labelled "Pure grape juice," one of those non-alcoholic beverages with which the teetotaler whips the devil around the stump; another glass would have made Shakers of us all, for the juice of the grape in this instance was about twenty-five per cent proof. If the good sisters supply their worthy brothers in faith with this stimulating cordial, it is not unlikely that life in the village is less monotonous than is commonly supposed. It certainly was calculated to add emphasis to the eccentricities of even a "Shaking Quaker."

Although the oldest and the wealthiest of all the socialistic communities, there are only about six thousand Shakers in the United States, less than one-fourth of what there were in former times.

At Mt. Lebanon, the first founded of the several societies in this country, there are seven families, or separate communities, each with its own home and buildings. The present membership is about one hundred and twenty, nearly all women, — scarcely enough men to provide the requisite deacons for each family.

Large and well-managed schools are provided to attract children from the outside world, and so recruit the diminishing ranks of the faithful; but while many girls remain, the boys steal away to the heathen world, where marriage is an institution.

Celibacy is the cardinal principle and the curse of Shakerism; it is slowly but surely bringing the sect to an end. It takes a lot of fanaticism to remain single, and fanaticism is in the sere and yellow leaf. In Massachusetts, where so many women are compelled to remain single, there ought to be many Shakers; there are a few, and Mt. Lebanon is just over the line.

Celibacy does not appeal strongly to men. A man is quite willing to live alone if it is not compulsory, but celibates cannot stand restraint; the bachelor is bound to have his own way — until he is married. Tell a man he may not marry, and he will; that he must marry, and he won't.

The sect which tries to get along with either too little or too much marriage is bound to peter out. There were John Noyes and Brigham Young. John founded the Oneida Community upon the proposition that everything should be in common, including husbands, wives, and children; from the broadest possible communism his community has regenerated into the closet of stock companies "limited," with a capital stock of seven hundred and fifty thousand dollars, a surplus of one hundred and fifty thousand, and only two hundred and nineteen stockholders.

In the palmy days of Mormonism the men could have as many wives as they could afford, — a scheme not without its practical advantages in the monotonous life of pioneer settlements, since it gave the women something to quarrel about and the men something to think about, thereby keeping both out of mischief, — but with the advent of civilization with its diverse interests, the men of Salt Lake, urged also by the law, are getting tired of more than one wife at a time, and the community will soon be absorbed and lost in the commonplace. The ancient theory of wives in multiples is giving place to the modern practice of wives in series.

The story is told that a dear Shaker brother once fell from grace and disappeared in the maelstrom of the carnal world; in a few years he came back as penitent as he was penniless, with strange accounts of how men had fleeced him of all he possessed save the clothes — none too desirable — on his back. Men were so scarce that the credulous sisters and charitable deacons voted to accept his tales as true and receive him once more into the fold.

It was in 1770, while in prison in England, that Ann Lee claimed to have had a great revelation concerning original sin, wherein it was revealed that a celibate life is a condition precedent to spiritual regeneration. Her revelation may have been biased by the fact that she herself was married, but not comfortably.

In 1773, on her release from prison, another revelation told her to go to America. Her husband did not sympathize with the celibacy proposition, left "Mother Ann," as she was then known, and went off with another woman who was unhampered by revelations. This was the beginning of desertions which have continued ever since, until the men are reduced to a corporal's guard.

The principles of the Shakers, barring celibacy, are sound and practical, and, so far as known, they live up to them quite faithfully. Like the original Oneida community, they believe in free criticism of one another in open meetings. They admit no one to the society unless he or she promises to make a full confession before others of every evil that can be recalled, — women confess to women, men to men; these requirements make it difficult to recruit their ranks. They are opposed to war and violence, do not vote, and do not permit corporal punishment. They pay their full share of public taxes and assessments and give largely in charity. Their buildings are well built and well kept, their farms and lands worked to the best advantage; in short, they are industrious and thrifty.

Communism is one of those dreams that come so often to the best of mankind and, lingering on through the waking hours, influence conduct. The sharp distinctions and inequalities of life seem so harsh and unjust; the wide intervals which separate those who have from those who have not seem so unfair, that in all ages and in all countries men have tried to devise schemes for social equality, — equality of power, opportunity, and achievement. Communism of some sort is one solution urged, — communism in property, communism in effort, communism in results, everything in common.

In 1840 Emerson wrote to Carlyle, "We are all a little wild here with numberless projects of social reform. Not a reading man but has a draft of a new community in his waistcoat pocket. I am gently mad myself, and am resolved to live cleanly. George Ripley is talking up a colony of agriculturists and scholars, with whom he threatens to take the field and book. One man renounces the use of animal food; another of coin; and another of domestic hired service; and another of the State; and on the whole we have a commendable share of reason and of hope."

Ripley did found his Brook Farm, and a lot of good people went and lived there — not Emerson; he was just a trifle too sane to be won over completely, but even he used to go into his own garden and dig in a socialistic way until his little boy warned him not to dig his foot.

That is the trouble with communism, those who dig are apt to dig their feet. It is easier to call a spade a spade than to use one. Men may be born free and equal, but if they are, they do not show it. From his first breath man is oppressed by the conditions of his existence, and life is a struggle with environment. Freedom and liberty are terms of relative not absolute value. The absolutism of the commune is oppression refined, each man must dig even if he digs his own foot. The plea of the anarchist for liberty is more consistent than the plea of the communist, — the one does demand a wild, lawless freedom for individual initiative; the other demands the very refinement of interference with liberty of mind and body.

The evolutionist looks on with philosophic indifference, knowing that what is to be will be, that the stream of tendency is not to be checked or swerved by vaporings, but moves irresistibly onward, though every thought, every utterance, every experiment, however wild, however visionary, has its effect.

We of the practical world sojourning in the Shaker village may commiserate the disciples of theory, but they are happy in their own way, — possibly happier in their seclusion and routine than we are in our hurly-burly and endless strife for social, commercial, and political advantages. Life is as settled and certain for them as it is unsettled and uncertain for us. No problems confront them; the everlasting query, "What shall we do tomorrow?" is never asked; plans for the coming summer do not disturb them; the seashore is far off; Paris and Monte Carlo are but places, vague and indistinct, the fairy tales of travellers; their city is the four walls of their home; their world the one long, silent, street of the village; their end the little graveyard beyond; it is all planned out, foreseen, and arranged.

Such a life is not without its charms, and it is small wonder that in all ages men of intellect have sought in some form of communistic association relief from the pressure of strenuous individualism. We may smile with condescension upon the busy sisters in their caps and gingham gowns, but, who knows, theirs may be the better lot.

Life with us is a good deal of an automobile race, — a lot of dust, dirt, and noise; explosions, accidents, and delays; something wrong most of the time; now a burst of headlong speed, then a jolt and sudden stop; or a creeping pace with disordered mechanism; no time to think of much except the machine; less time to see anything except the road immediately ahead; strife to pass others; reckless indifference to life and limb; one long, mad contest for success and notoriety, ending for the most part in some sort of disaster, — possibly a sea of flame.

If we possessed any sense of grim, sardonic humor, we would appreciate how ridiculous is the life we lead, how utterly absurd is our waste of time, our dissipation of the few days and hours vouchsafed us. We are just so many cicadas drumming out the hours and disappearing. We have abundance of wit, and a good deal of humor of a superficial kind, but the penetrating vision of a Socrates, a Voltaire, a Carlyle is denied the most of us, and we take ourselves and our accustomed pursuits most seriously.

On our way back from the village we stopped at the birthplace of Samuel Tilden, — an old-fashioned white frame house, situated in the very fork of the roads, and surrounded by tall trees. Not far away is the cemetery, where a stone sarcophagus contains the remains of a man who was very able if not very great.

Probably not fifty people in the United States, aside from those living in the neighborhood, know where Tilden was born. We did not until we came abruptly upon the house and were told; probably not a dozen could tell exactly where he is buried. Such is fame. And yet this man, in the belief of most of his countrymen, was chosen president, though never seated; he was governor of New York and a vital force in the politics and public life of his times, — now forgotten.

What a disappointment it must have been to come so near and yet miss the presidency. Before 1880 came around, his own party had so far forgotten him that he was scarcely mentioned for renomination, — though Tilden decrepit was incomparably stronger than Hancock "the superb." It was hard work enthusing over "Hancock and Hooray" after "Tilden and Reform;" the latter cry had substance, the former was just fustian.

The Democratic party is as iconoclastic as the Republican is reverential. The former loves to pick flaws in its idols and dash them to pieces; the latter, with stolid conservatism, clings loyally to its mediocrities. The latter could have elected Bryan, the former could not; the Democratic stomach is freaky and very squeamish; it swallows many things but digests few; the ostrich-like Republican organ has never been known to reject anything.

Republicans swear stanchly by every president they have ever elected. Democrats abandoned Tilden and spurned Cleveland, the only two men they have come within a thousand miles of electing in ten campaigns. The lesson of well-nigh half a century makes no impression, the blind are leading the blind.

It is a far cry from former leaders such as Tilden, Hewitt, Bayard, and Cleveland to those of today; a party which seeks its candidate among the populists of Nebraska courts defeat. The two nominations of Bryan mark low level in the political tide; it is not conceivable that a great political party could sink lower; for less of a statesman and more of a demagogue does not exist. The one great opportunity the little man had to show some ability as a leader was when the treaty of Paris was being fiercely debated at Washington; the sentiment of his party and the best men of the country were against the purchase of the Philippines; but this cross-roads politician, who could not see beyond the tip of his nose, hastened to Washington, played into the hands of the jingoes by persuading the wiser men of his own party—men who should not have listened to him—to withdraw their opposition.

Bryan had two opportunities to exhibit qualities of statesmanship in the beginning of the war with Spain, and in the discussion of the treaty of Paris; he missed both. So far as the war was concerned, he never had an idea beyond a little cheap renown as a paper colonel of volunteers; so far as the treaty was concerned, he made the unpardonable blunder of playing into the hands of his opponents, and leaving the sound and conservative sentiment of the country without adequate leadership in Washington.

While we were curiously looking at the Tilden homestead, an old man came walking slowly down the road, a rake over his shoulder, one leg of his patched trousers stuck in a boot-top, a suspender missing, his old straw hat minus a goodly portion of its crown. He stopped, leaned upon his rake, and looked at us inquisitively, then remarked in drawling tone,

"I know'd Sam Tilden."

"Indeed!"

"Yes, I know'd him; he was a great man."

"You are a Democrat?"

"I wuz, but ain't now," pensively.

"Why ar'n't you?"

"Well, you see, I wuz allus a rock-ribbed Jacksonian fr'm a boy; seed the ole gen'ral onc't, an' I voted for Douglas an' Seymore. I skipped Greeley, fur he warn't no Dem'crat; an' I voted fur Tilden an' Hancock an' Cleveland; but when it come to votin' fur a cyclone fr'm N'braska,—jest wind an' nothin' more,—I kicked over the traces."

"Then you don't believe in the divine ratio of sixteen to one?"

"Young man, silver an' gold come out'r the ground, jes' lik' corn an' wheat. When you kin make two bush'ls corn wu'th a bush'l wheat by law an' keep 'em there, you can fix the rasho 'twixt silver an' gold, an' not before," and the old man shouldered his rake and wandered on up the road.

Before leaving the birthplace of Tilden, it is worth noting that for forty years every candidate favored by Tammany has been ignominiously defeated; the two candidates bitterly opposed by the New York machine were successful. It is to the credit of the party that no Democrat can be elected president unless he is the avowed and unrelenting foe of corruption within and without the ranks.

The farmer with whom we were staying had earlier in the summer a flock of sixty young and promising turkeys; of the lot but twenty were left, and one of them was moping about as his forty brothers and sisters had moped before, ready to die.

"Ah, he'll go with the others," said the farmer. "Raising turkeys is a ticklish job; today they're scratching gravel for all they're worth; tomorrow they mope around an' die; no telling what's the matter."

"Suppose we give that turkey some whiskey and water; it may help."

"Can't do any harm, fur he'll die anyway; it's a waste of medicine."

Soaking some bread in good, strong Scotch, diluted with very little water, we gave the turkey what was equivalent to a teaspoonful. The bird did not take unkindly to the mixture. It had been standing about all day first on one leg, then on another, with eyes half closed and head turned feebly to one side. In a few moments the effect of the whiskey became apparent; the half-grown bird could no longer stand on one leg, but used both, placing them well apart for support. It began to show signs of animation, peering about with first one eye and then the other; with great gravity and deliberation it made its way to the centre of the road and looked about for gravel; fixing its eye upon an attractive little pebble it aimed for it, missed it by about two inches and rolled in the dust; by this time the other turkeys were staring in amazement; slowly pulling itself together he shook the dust from his feathers, cast a scornful eye upon the crowd about him and looked again for the pebble; there it was within easy shot; taking good aim with one eye closed he made another lunge, ploughed his head into the dust, making a complete somersault. By this time the two old turkeys were attracted by the unusual excitement; making their way through the throng of youngsters, they gazed for a moment upon the downfall of one of their progeny, and then giving vent to their indignation in loud cries pounced upon their tipsy offspring and pecked him until he struggled upright and staggered away. The last we saw of the young scapegrace he was smoothing his ruffled plumage before a shining milk-pail and apparently admonishing his unsteady double. It is worth recording that the turkey was better the next day, and lived, as we were afterwards told, to a ripe old Thanksgiving age.

The new steering-head came early the next morning; in thirty minutes it was in place. Our host and valley hostess were then given their first automobile ride; she, womanlike, took the speed, sudden turns, and strange sensations more coolly than he. As a rule, women and children are more fearless than men in an automobile; this is not because they have more courage, but men realize more vividly the things that might happen, whereas women and children simply feel the exhilaration of the speed without thinking of possible disasters.

We went down the road at a thirty-mile clip, made a quick turn at the four corners, and were back almost before the dust we raised had settled.

"That's something like," said our host; "but the old horse is a good enough automobile for me."

The hold-all was soon strapped in place, and at half-past nine we were off for Pittsfield.

Passing the Tilden homestead, we soon began the ascent of the mountain, following the superb new State road.

The old road was through the Shaker village and contained grades which rendered it impossible for teams to draw any but the lightest loads. It was only when market conditions were very abnormal that the farmers in the valley would draw their hay, grain, and produce to Pittsfield.

The new State road winds around and over the mountain at a grade nowhere exceeding five per cent and averaging a little over four. It is a broad macadam, perfectly constructed.

In going up this easy and perfectly smooth ascent for some six or seven miles, the disadvantage of having no intermediate-speed gears was forcibly illustrated, for the grade was just too stiff for the high-speed gear, and yet so easy that the engine tended to race on the low, but we had to make the entire ascent on the hill-climbing gear at a rate of about four or five miles an hour; an intermediate-gear would have carried us up at twelve or fifteen miles per hour.

CHAPTER 12

Pittsfield

"THE COURT CONSIDERS THE MATTER"
In Pittsfield the machine frightened a lawyer, — not a woman, or a child, or a horse, or a donkey, — but just a lawyer; to be sure, there was nothing to indicate he was a lawyer, and still less that he was unusually timid of his kind, therefore no blame could attach for failing to distinguish him from men less nervous.

That he was frightened, no one who saw him run could deny; that he was needlessly frightened, seemed equally plain; that he was chagrined when bystanders laughed at his exhibition, was highly probable.

Now law is the business of a lawyer; it is his refuge in trouble and at the same time his source of revenue; and it is a poor lawyer who cannot make his refuge pay a little something every time it affords him consolation for real or fancied injury.

In this case the lawyer collected exactly sixty cents' worth of consolation, — two quarters and a dime, the price of two lunches and a cup of coffee, or a dozen "Pittsfield Stogies," if there be so fragrant a brand; — the lay mind cannot grasp the possibilities of two quarters and a ten-cent piece in the strong and resourceful grasp of a Pittsfield lawyer. In these thrifty New England towns one always gets a great many pennies in change; small money is the current coin; great stress is set upon a well-worn quarter, and a dime is precious in the sight of the native.

It so happened that just about the time of our arrival, the machinery of justice in and about Pittsfield was running a little wild anyway.

In an adjoining township, on the same day, ex-President Cleveland, who was whiling away time in the philosophic pursuit of fishing, was charged with catching and retaining longer than the law allowed a bass which was a quarter of an inch under the legal limit of eight inches. Now in the excitement of the moment that bass no doubt felt like a whale to the great man, and as it neared the surface, after the manner of its kind, it of course looked as long as a pickerel; then, too; the measly fish was probably a silver bass, and once in the boat shrunk a quarter of an inch, just to get the eminent old Democrat in trouble.

At all events, the friend who was along gallantly claimed the bass as his, appeared in the Great Barrington district court, and paid a fine of two dollars.

Now these things are characteristic of the place, daubs of local coloring; the summer resident upon whom the provincials thrive is not disturbed; but the stranger who is within the gates, who is just passing through, from whom no money in the way of small purchases and custom is to be expected, he is legitimate plunder, even though he be so distinguished a stranger as an ex-President of the United States.

A local paper related the fishing episode as follows:

"Ex-President Grover Cleveland, who is spending the summer in Tyringham, narrowly escaped being arrested at Lake Garfield, in Monterey, Thursday afternoon. As it was, he received a verbal summons to appear in the Great Barrington district court this morning and answer the charge of illegal fishing. But when the complainants learned who the distinguished person was with whom they were dealing, they let drop the matter of swearing out a warrant, and in Mr. Cleveland's place appeared Cassius C. Scranton, of Monterey.

"He pleaded guilty to catching a bass less than eight inches in length, which is the minimum allowed by law, and was fined two dollars by Judge Sanford, but as Mr. Cleveland said that he caught the fish, there is still a good deal of doubt among the residents of southern Berkshire as to which one was actually guilty. However, if the hero of the Hawaiian enterprise was the unlucky angler who caught the bass, he was relieved of the unpleasant notoriety of being summoned into court on a warrant by the very charitable act of Mr. Scranton, of Monterey, who will forever go down in the history of that town as the stalwart defender of the ex-president."

It is not conceivable that such a ridiculous display of impecunious justice would be made elsewhere in the country. In the South the judge would dismiss the complainant or pay the fine himself; in the West he would be mobbed if he did not. New York would find a tactful and courteous way of avoiding the semblance of an arrest or the imposition of a fine; but in thrifty Massachusetts, and in thrice thrifty Great Barrington, and in twice thrice thrifty Pittsfield, pennies count, are counted, and most conscientiously received and receipted for by those who set the wheels of justice in motion.

North Street is broad and West Street is broad, and there is abundance of room for man and beast.

At the hour in question there were no women, children, or horses in the street; the crossings were clear save for a young man with a straw hat, whose general appearance betrayed no sign of undue timidity. He was on the far crossing, sixty or seventy feet distant. When the horn was sounded for the turn down into West Street, he turned, gave one look at the machine, jumped, and ran. In a few moments the young man with the straw hat came to the place where the machine had stopped. He was followed by a short, stubby little friend with a sandy beard, who, while apparently acting as second, threatened each moment to take the matter into his own hands and usurp the place of principal.

Straw Hat was placable and quite disposed to accept an expression of regret that fright had been occasioned.

Sandy Beard would not have it so, and urged Straw Hat to make a complaint.

Straw Hat spurred on his flagging indignation and asked for a card.

Sandy Beard told Straw Hat not to be deterred by soft words and civility, and promised to stand by him, or rather back of him; whereupon something like the following might have occurred.

Sandy Beard. — Then you know what is to be done?

Straw Hat. — Not I, upon my soul!

Sandy Beard. — We wear no clubs here, but you understand me.

Straw Hat. — What! arrest him.

Sandy Beard. — Why to be sure; what can I mean else?

Straw Hat. — But he has given me no provocation.

Sandy Beard. — Now, I think he has given you the greatest provocation in the world. Can a man commit a more heinous offence against another than to frighten him? Ah! by my soul, it is a most unpardonable breach of something.

Straw Hat. — Breach of something! Ay, ay; but is't a breach of the peace? I have no acquaintance with this man. I never saw him before in my life.

Sandy Beard. — That's no argument at all; he has the less right to take such a liberty.

Straw Hat. — Gad, that's true. I grow full of anger, Sir Sandy! fire ahead! Odds, writs and warrants! I find a man may have a good deal of valor in him, and not know it! But couldn't I contrive to have a little right on my side?

Sandy Beard. — What the devil signifies right when your courage is concerned. Do you think Verges, or my little Dogberry ever inquired where the right lay? No, by my soul; they drew their writs, and left the lazy justice of the peace to settle the right of it.

Straw Hat. — Your words are a grenadier's march to my heart! I believe courage must be catching! I certainly do feel a kind of valor rising as it were, — a kind of courage, as I may say. Odds, writs and warrants! I'll complain directly.

(With apologies to Sheridan.)

And the pair went off to make their complaint.

Suppose each had been given then and there the sixty cents he afterwards received and duly receipted for, would it have saved time and trouble? Who knows? but the afternoon diversion would have been lost.

In a few moments an officer quite courteously — refreshing contrast — notified me that complaint was in process of making.

I found the chief of police with a copy of the city ordinance trying to draw some sort of a complaint that would fit the extraordinary case, for the charge was not the usual one, that the machine was going at an unlawful speed, but that a lawyer had been frightened; to find the punishment that would fit that crime was no easy task.

The ordinance is liberal, — ten miles an hour; and the young man and his mentor had not said the speed of the automobile was greater than the law allowed, hence the dilemma of the chief; but we discussed a clause which provided that vehicles should not be driven through the streets in a manner so as to endanger public travel, and he thought the complaint would rest on that provision.

However lacking the bar of Pittsfield may be in the amenities of life, the bench is courtesy itself. There was no court until next day; but calling at the judge's very delightful home, which happens to be on one of the interesting old streets of the town, he said he would come down and hear the matter at two o'clock, so I could get away that afternoon.

The first and wisest impulse of the automobilist is to pay whatever fine is imposed and go on, but frightening a lawyer is not an everyday occurrence. I once frightened a pair of army mules; but a lawyer, — the experience was too novel to let pass lightly. The game promised to be worth the candle.

The scene shifts to a dingy little room in the basement of the courthouse; present, Straw Hat and Sandy Beard, with populace.

To corroborate — wise precaution on the part of a lawyer in his own court—their story, they bring along a volunteer witness in overalls, — the three making a trio hard to beat.

Straw Hat takes the stand and testifies he is an unusually timid man, and was most frightened to death.

Sandy Beard's testimony is both graphic and corroborative.

The witness in overalls, with some embellishments of his own, supports Sandy Beard.

The row of bricks is complete.

The court removes a prop by remarking that the ordinance speed has not been exceeded.

The bricks totter.

Whereupon, Sandy Beard now takes the matter into his own hands, and, ignoring the professional acquirements of his principal, addresses the court and urges the imposition of a fine. — a fine being the only satisfaction, and source of immediate revenue, conceivable to Sandy Beard.

Meanwhile Straw Hat is silent; the witness in overalls is perturbed.

The court considers the matter, and says "the embarrassing feature of the case is that it has yet to be shown that the defendant was going at a rate exceeding ten miles an hour, and upon this point the witnesses did not agree. There was evidence tending to prove the machine was going ten miles an hour, but that would not lead to conviction under the first clause of the ordinance; but there is another clause which says that a machine must not be run in such a manner as to endanger or inconvenience public travel. What is detrimental to public travel? Does it mean to run it so as not to frighten a man of nerve like the chief of police, or some timid person? It is urged that not one man in a thousand would have been frightened like Mr. —— ; but a man is bound to run his machine in the streets so as to frighten no one, therefore the defendant is fined five dollars and costs."

The fine is duly paid, and Messrs. Straw Hat, Sandy Beard, and Overalls, come forward, receive and receipt for sixty cents each.

Their wrath was appeased, their wounded feelings soothed, their valor satisfied, — one dollar and eighty cents for the bunch.

CHAPTER 13

Through Massachusetts

IN LENOX

There are several roads out of Pittsfield to Springfield, and if one asks a half-dozen citizens, who pretend to know, which is the best, a half-dozen violently conflicting opinions will be forthcoming.

The truth seems to be that all the roads are pretty good, — that is, they are all very hilly and rather soft. One expects the hills, and must put up with the sand. It is impossible to get to Springfield, which is far on the other side of the mountains, without making some stiff grades, — few grades so bad as Nelson's Hill out of Peekskill, or worse than Pride's Hill near Fonda; in fact, the grades through the Berkshires are no worse than many short stiff grades that are to be found in any rolling country, but there are more of them, and occasionally the road is rough or soft, making it hard going.

The road commonly recommended as the more direct is by way of Dalton and Hinsdale, following as closely as possible the line of the Boston and Albany; this winds about in the valleys and is said to be very good.

We preferred a more picturesque though less travelled route. We wished to go through Lenox, some six or seven miles to the south, and if anything a little to the west, and therefore out of our direct course.

The road from Pittsfield to Lenox is a famous drive, one of the wonders of that little world. It is not bad, neither is it good. Compared with the superb State road over the mountain, it is a trail over a prairie. As a matter of fact, it is just a broad, graded, and somewhat improved highway, too rough for fast speed and comfort, and on the Saturday morning in question dust was inches deep.

The day was fine, the country beautiful; hills everywhere, hills so high they were almost mountains. The dust of summer was on the foliage, a few late blossoms lingered by the roadside, but for the most part flowers had turned to seeds, and seeds were ready to fall. The fields were in stubble, hay in the mow and straw in the stack. The green of the hills was deeper in hue, the valleys were ripe for autumn.

People were flocking to the Berkshires from seashore and mountains; the "season" was about to begin in earnest; hotels were filled or rapidly filling, and Lenox — dear, peaceful little village in one of nature's fairest hollows — was most enticing as we passed slowly through, stopping once or twice to make sure of our very uncertain way.

The slowest automobile is too fast for so delightful a spot as Lenox. One should amble through on a palfrey, or walk, or, better still, pass not through at all, but tarry and dream the days away until the last leaves are off the trees. But the habit of the automobile is infectious, one goes on and on in spite of all attractions, the appeals of nature, the protests of friends. Ulysses should have whizzed by the Sirens in an auto. The Wandering Jew, if still on his rounds, should buy a machine; it will fit his case to a nicety; his punishment will become a habit; he will join an automobile club, go on an endurance contest, and, in the brief moments allowed him for rest and oiling up, will swap stories with the boys.

With a sigh of relief, one finishes a long day's run, thinking it will suffice for many a day to come; the evening is scarce over before elfin suggestions of possible rides for the morrow are floating about in the air, and when morning comes the automobile is taken out, — very much as the toper who has sworn off the night before takes his morning dram, — it just can't be helped.

Our way lay over October Mountain by a road not much frequented. In the morning's ride we did not meet a trap of any kind or a rider, — something quite unusual in that country of riders and drivers. The road seemed to cling to the highest hills, and we climbed up and up for hours. Only once was the grade so steep that we were obliged to dismount. We passed through no village until we reached the other side, but every now and then we would come to a little clearing with two or three houses, possibly a forlorn store and a silent blacksmith shop; these spots seemed even more lonely and deserted than the woods themselves. Man is so essentially a gregarious animal that to come upon a lone house in a wilderness is more depressing than the forests. Nature is never alone; it knows no solitude; it is a mighty whole, each part of which is in constant communication with every other part. Nature needs no telephone; from time immemorial it has used wireless telegraphy in a condition of perfection unknown to man. Every morning Mount Blanc sends a message to

Pike's Peak, and it sends it on over the waters to Fujisan. The bosom of the earth thrills with nervous energy; the air is charged with electric force; the blue ether of the universe throbs with motion. Nature knows no environment; but man is fettered, a spirit in a cage, a mournful soul that seeks companionship in misery. Solitude is a word unknown to nature's vocabulary. The deepest recesses of the forest teem with life and joyousness until man appears, then they are filled with solitude. The wind-swept desert is one of nature's play-grounds until man appears, then it is barren with solitude. The darkest mountain cavern echoes with nature's laughter until man appears, then it is hollow with solitude.

Instead of coming out at Becket as we expected, we found ourselves way down near Otis and West Otis, and passed through North Blandford and Blandford to Fairfield, where we struck the main road.

We stopped for dinner at a small village a few miles from Westfield. There was but one store, but it kept a barrel of stove gasoline in an apple orchard. The gasoline was good, but the gallon measure into which it was drawn had been used for oil, varnish, turpentine, and every liquid a country store is supposed to keep—not excepting molasses. It was crusted with sediment and had a most evil smell. Needless to say the measure was rejected; but that availed little, since the young clerk poured the gasoline back into the barrel to draw it out again into a cleaner receptacle.

The gasoline for sale at country stores is usually all right, but it is handled in all sorts of receptacles; the only safe way is to ask for a bright and new dipper and let the store-keeper guess at the measure.

At Westfield the spark began to give trouble; the machine was very slow in starting, as if the batteries were weak; but that could not be, for one set was fresh and the other by no means exhausted. A careful examination of every connection failed to disclose any breaks in the circuit, and yet the spark was of intermittent strength, — now good, now weak.

When there is anything wrong with an automobile, there is but one thing to do, and that is find the source of the trouble and remedy it. The temptation is to go on if the machine starts up unexpectedly. We yielded to the temptation, and went on as soon as the motor started; the day was so fine and we were so anxious to get to Worcester that we started with the motor, knowing all the time that whatever made the motor slow to start would, in all likelihood, bring us to a stand-still before very long; the evil moment, possibly the evil hour, may be postponed, but seldom the evil day.

At two o'clock we passed through Springfield, stopping only a moment at the hotel to inquire for mail. Leaving Springfield we followed the main road towards Worcester, some fifty miles away. The road is winding and over a rolling country, but for the most part very good. The grades are not steep, there are some sandy spots, but none so soft as to materially interfere with good speed. There are many stretches of good gravel, and here and there a piece—a sample—of State road, perfectly laid macadam, with signs all along requesting persons not to drive in the centre of the highway,—this is to save the road from the hollows and ruts that horses and narrow-tired wagons invariably make, and in which the water stands, ultimately wearing the macadam through. We could not see that the slightest attention was paid to the notices. Everybody kept the middle of the road, such is the improvidence of men; the country people grumble at the expense of good roads, and then take the surest way to ruin them.

While it is true that the people in the first instance grumble at the prospective cost of these well-made State roads, no sooner are they laid than their very great value is appreciated, and good roads sentiment becomes rampant. The farmer who has worn out horses, harness, wagons, and temper in getting light loads to market over heavy roads is quick to appreciate the very material advantage and economy of having highways over which one horse can pull as much as two under the old sandy, rough, and muddy conditions.

A good road may be the making of a town, and it increases the value of all abutting property. Already the question is commonly asked when a farm is offered for sale or rent, "Is it on a State road?" Lots will not sell in cities unless all improvements are in; soon farmers will not be able to sell unless the highways are improved.

One good thing about the automobile, it does not cut up the surface of a macadam or gravel road as do steel tires and horseshoes.

At the outskirts of the little village of West Brookfield we came to a stand-still; the spark disappeared,—or rather from a large, round, fat spark it dropped to an insignificant little blue sparklet that would not explode a squib.

The way the spark acted with either or both batteries on indicated pretty strongly that the trouble was in the coil; but it is so seldom a coil goes wrong that everything was looked over, but no spark of any size was to be had, therefore there was nothing to do but cast about for a place to spend the night, for it was then dark.

As good luck would have it, we were almost in front of a large, comfortable, old-fashioned house where they took summer boarders; as the season was drawing to a close, there was plenty of room and they were glad to take us in. The machine was pushed into a shed, everybody assisting with the readiness ever characteristic of sympathetic on-lookers.

The big, clean, white rooms were most inviting; the homely New England supper of cold meats and hot rolls seemed under the circumstances a feast for a king, and as we sat in front of the house in the evening, and looked across the highway to a little lake just beyond and heard the croaking of the frogs, the chirping of crickets, and the many indistinguishable sounds of night, we were not sorry the machine had played us false exactly when and where it did.

The automobile plays into the hands of Morpheus, the drowsy god follows in its wake, sure of his victims. No sleep is dreamless. It is pretty difficult to exhaust the three billions of cells of the central nervous system so that all require rest, but ten hours on an automobile in the open air, speeding along like the wind most of the time, will come nearer putting all those cells to sleep than any exercise heretofore discovered. The fatigue is normal, pervasive, and persuasive, and it is pretty hard to recall any dream on waking.

It was Sunday morning, September 1, and raining, a soft, drizzly downpour, that had evidently begun early in the night and kept up — or rather down — steadily. It was a good morning to remain indoors and read; but there was that tantalizing machine challenging combat; then, too, Worcester was but eighteen or twenty miles away, and at Worcester we expected to find letters and telegrams.

A young and clever electrician across the way came over, bringing an electric bell, with which we tested the dry cells, finding them in good condition. We then examined the connections and ran the trouble back to the coil. There was plenty of current and plenty of voltage, but only a little blue spark, which could be obtained equally well with the coil in or out of the circuit, and yet the coil did not show a short circuit, but before we finished our tests the spark suddenly appeared.

Again, it would have been better to remain and find the trouble; but as there was no extra coil to be had in the village, it seemed fairly prudent to start on and get as far as possible. Possibly the coil would hold out to Worcester; anyway, the road is a series of villages, some larger than Brookfield, and a coil might be found at one of them.

When within two miles of Spencer the spark gave out again; this time no amount of coaxing would bring it back, so there was nothing to do but appeal to a farmer for a pair of horses to pull the machine into his yard. The assistance was most kindly given, though the day was Sunday, and for him, his men and his animals, emphatically a day of rest.

Only twice on the entire trip were horses attached to the machine; but a sparking coil is absolutely essential, and when one gives out it is pretty hard to make repairs on the road. In case of necessity a coil may be unwound, the trouble discovered and remedied, but that is a tedious process. It was much easier to leave the machine for the night, run into Worcester on the trolley which passed along the same road, and bring out a new coil in the morning.

Monday happened to be Labor Day, and it was only after much trouble that a place was found open where electrical supplies could be purchased. In addition o a coil, the electrician took cut some thoroughly insulated double cable wire; the wiring of the machine had been so carelessly done and with such light, cheap wire that it seemed a good opportunity to rewire throughout.

The electrician — a very competent and quick workman he proved to be — was so sure the trouble could not be in the coil that he did not wish to carry out a new one.

When ready to start, we found the trolley line blocked by a Labor Day parade that was just beginning to move. The procession was unusually long on account of striking trades unionists, who turned out in force. As each section of strikers passed, the electrician explained the cause of their strike, the number of men out, and the length of time they had been out.

It seemed too bad that big, brawny, intelligent men could find no better way of adjusting differences with employers than by striking.

A strike is an expensive luxury. Three parties are losers, — the community in general by being deprived for the time being of productive forces; the employers by loss on capital invested; the employees by loss of wages. The loss to the community, while very real, is little felt. Employers, as a rule, are prepared to stand their losses with equanimity; in fact, when trade is dull, or when an employer desires to make changes in his business, a strike is no inconvenience at all; but the men are the real losers, and especially those with families and with small homes unpaid for; no one can measure their losses, for it may mean the savings of a lifetime. It frequently does mean a change in character from an industrious, frugal, contented workman with everything to live for, to a shiftless and discontented man with nothing to live for but agitation and strife.

It is easy to acquire the strike habit, and impossible to throw it off. A first strike is more dangerous than a first drink; it makes a profound and ineradicable impression. To quit work for the first time at the command of some central organization is an experience so novel that no man can do it without being affected; he will never again be the same steady and indefatigable workman; the spirit of unrest creeps in, the spirit of discontent closely follows; his life is changed; though he never goes through another strike, he can never forget his first.

In the long run it does not matter much which side wins, the effect is very much the same, — strikes are bound to follow strikes. Warfare is so natural to men that it is difficult to declare a lasting peace. But some day the men themselves will see that strikes are far more disastrous to them than to any other class, and they will devise other ways and means; they will use the strength of their organizations to better advantage; above all, they will relegate to impotency the professional organizers and agitators who retain their positions by fomenting strife.

It is singular that workmen do not take a lesson from their shrewder employers, who, if they have organizations of their own, never confer upon any officer or committee of idlers the power to control the trade. An organization of employers is always controlled by those most actively engaged in the business, and not by coteries of paid idlers; no central committee of men, with nothing to do but make trouble, can involve a whole trade in costly controversies. The strength of the employer lies in the fact that each man consults first his own interest, and if the action of the body bids fair to injure his individual interests he not only protests, but threatens to withdraw; the employer cannot be cowed by any association of which he is a member; but the employee is cowed by his union, — that is the essential difference between the two. An association of employers is a union of independent and aggressive units, and the action of the association must meet the approval of each of these units or disruption will follow.

Workingmen do not seem to appreciate the value of the unit; they are attracted by masses. They seem to think strength lies only in members; but that is the keynote of militantism, the death-knell of individualism. The real, the only strength of a union lies in the silent, unconsulted units; now and then they rise up and act and the union accomplishes something; for the most part they do not act, but are blindly led, and the union accomplishes nothing.

It was interesting to hear the comments of the intelligent young mechanic as the different trades passed by.

"Those fellows are out on a sympathetic strike; no grievance at all, plenty of work and good wages, but just out because they are told to come out; big fools, I say, to be pulled about by the nose.

"There are the plumbers; their union makes more trouble than any other in the building trades; they are always looking for trouble, and manage to find it when no one else can.

"Unions are all right for bachelors who can afford to loaf, but they are pretty hard on the married man with a family.

"What's gained in a strike is lost in the fight.

"What's the use of staying out three months to get a ten per cent raise for nine? It doesn't pay.

"Wages have been going up for two hundred years. I can't see that the strike has advanced the rate of increase any.

"These fellows have tried to monopolize Labor Day; they don't want any non-union man in the parade; the people will not stand for that very long; labor is labor whether union or non-union, and the great majority of workingmen in this country are not members of any union."

The parade, like all things good, came to an end, and we took the trolley for the place where the automobile had been left.

On arriving we took out the dry cells, tested each one, and then rewired the carriage complete and in a manner to defy rain, sand, and oil. The difficulty, however, was in the coil. Apparently the motion of the vehicle had worn the insulation through at some point inside. The new coil, a common twelve-inch coil, worked well, giving a good, hot spark.

The farmer who had so kindly pulled the machine in the day before would accept nothing for his trouble, and was, as most farmers are, exceedingly kind. It is embarrassing to call upon strangers for assistance which means work and inconvenience for them, and then have them positively decline all compensation.

The ride into Worcester was a fast one over good gravel and macadam.

Immediately after luncheon we started for Boston. Every foot of the road in from Worcester is good hard gravel and the ride is most delightful. As it was a holiday and the highway was comparatively free of traffic, we travelled along faster than usual.

It was our intention to follow the main road through Shrewsbury, Southborough, Framingham, and Wellesley, but though man proposes, in the suburbs of Boston Providence disposes. About Southborough we lost our road, and were soon angling to the northeast through the Sudburys. So far as the road itself was concerned the change was for the better, for, while there would be stretches which were not gravelled, the country was more interesting than along the main highway.

The old "Worcester Turnpike" is Boyleston Street in Boston and through Brookline to the Newtons, where it becomes plain Worcester Street and bears that name westward through Wellesley and Natick.

The trolley line out of Worcester is through Shrewsbury and Northborough to Marlborough, then a turn almost due south to Southborough, then east to Framingham, southeast to South Framingham, east through Natick to Wellesley, northeast through Wellesley Hills to Newton, then direct through Brookline into Boston.

The road, it will be noted, is far from straight, and it is at the numerous forks and turns one is apt to go astray unless constant inquiries are made.

At Marlborough we kept on to the east towards Waltham instead of turning to the south for Southborough. It is but a few miles out of the way from Marlborough to Concord and into Boston by way of Lexington; or, if the road through Wellesley and Newton is followed, it is worth while to turn from Wellesley Hills to Norembega Park for the sake of stopping a few moments on the spot where Norembega Tower confidently proclaims the discovery of America and the founding of a fortified place by the Norsemen nearly five hundred years before Columbus sailed out of the harbor of Palos.

Having wandered from the old turnpike, we thought we would go by Concord and Lexington, but did not. The truth is the automobile is altogether too fast a conveyance for the suburbs of Boston, which were laid out by cows for the use of pedestrians. There are an infinite number of forks, angles, and turnings, and by a native on foot short cuts can be made to any objective point, but the automobile passes a byway before it is seen. Directions are given but not followed, because turns and obscure crossroads are passed at high speed and unobserved.

Everyone is most obliging in giving directions, but the directions run about like this:

"To Concord? — yes, — let me see; — do you know the Old Sudbury road? — No! — strangers? — ah! that's too bad, for if you don't know the

roads it will be hard telling you—but let me see;—if you follow this road
about a mile, you will come to a brick store and a watering trough,—take
the turn to the left there;—I think that is the best road, or you can take
a turn this side, but if I were you I would take the road at the watering
trough;—from there it is about eight miles, and I think you make three
turns,—but you better inquire, for if you don't know the roads it is pretty
hard to direct you."

"We follow this road straight ahead to the brick store and trough, that's
easy."

"Well, the road is not exactly straight, but if you bear to the right, then
take the second left hand fork, you'll be all right."

All of which things we most faithfully performed, and yet we got no
nearer that day than "about eight miles farther to Concord."

In circling about we came quite unexpectedly upon the old "Red Horse"
tavern, now the "Wayside Inn." We brought the machine to a stop and
gazed long and lovingly at the ancient hostelry which had given shelter
to famous men for nearly two hundred years, and where congenial spirits
gathered in Longfellow's days and the imaginary "Tales of a Wayside Inn"
were exchanged.

The mellow light of the setting sun warmed the time-worn structure
with a friendly glow. The sign of the red horse rampant creaked mournfully as it swung slowly to and fro in the gentle breeze; with palsied arms
and in cracked tones the old inn seemed to bid us stay and rest beneath
its sheltering eaves. Washington and Hamilton and Lafayette, Emerson
and Hawthorne and Longfellow had entered that door, eaten and drunk
within those humble walls,—the great in war, statecraft, and literature
had been its guests; like an old man it lives with its memories, recalls the
associations of its youth and prime, but slumbers oblivious to the present.

The old inn was so fascinating that we determined to come back in a
few days and spend at least a night beneath its roof. The shadows were
so rapidly lengthening that we had to hurry on.

Crossing the Charles River near Auburndale a sight of such bewitching
beauty met our astonished gaze that we stopped to make inquiries. Above
and below the bridge the river was covered with gayly decorated canoes
which were being paddled about by laughing and singing young people.
The brilliant colors of the decorations, the pretty costumes, the background of (lark water, the shores lined with people and equipages, the
bridge so crowded we could hardly get through, made a never-to-be-

forgotten picture. It was just a holiday canoe-meet, and hundreds of the small, frail craft were darting about upon the surface of the water like so many pretty dragon-flies. The automobile seemed such an intrusion, a drone of prose in a burst of poetry, the discord of machinery in a sylvan symphony.

We stopped a few moments at Lasell Seminary in Auburndale, where old associations were revived by my Companion over a cup of tea. A girl's school is a mysterious place; there is an atmosphere of suppressed mischief, of things threatened but never quite committed, of latent possibilities, and still more latent impossibilities. In a boy's school mischief is evident and rampant; desks, benches, and walls are whittled and defaced with all the wanton destructiveness of youth; buildings and fences show marks of contact with budding manhood; but boys are so openly and notoriously mischievous that no apprehension is felt, for the worst is ever realized; but those in command of a school of demure and saintly girls must feel like men handling dynamite, uncertain what will happen next; the stolen pie, the hidden sweets, the furtive note are indications of the infinite subtlety of the female mind.

From Auburndale the boulevard leads into Commonwealth Avenue and the run is fine.

It was about seven o'clock when we reached the Hotel Touraine, and a little later when the machine was safely housed in an automobile station, — a part of an old railway depot.

A few days in Boston and on the North Shore afforded a welcome change.

Through Beverly and Manchester the signs "Automobiles not allowed" at private roadways are numerous; they are the rule rather than the exception. One young man had a machine up there, but found himself so ostracized he shipped it away. No machines are allowed on the grounds of the Essex Country Club.

No man with the slightest consideration for the comfort and pleasure of others would care to keep and use a machine in places where so many women and children are riding and driving. The charm of the North Shore and the Berkshires lies largely in the opportunities afforded for children to be out with their ponies, girls with their carts, and women with horses too spirited to stand unusual sights and sounds. One automobile may terrorize the entire little community; in fact, one machine will spread terror where many would not.

It is quite difficult enough to drive a machine carefully through such resorts, without driving about day after day to the discomfort of every resident.

In a year or two all will be changed; the people who own summer homes will themselves own and use automobiles; the horses will see so many that little notice will be taken, but the pioneers of the sport will have an unenviable time.

A good half-day's work was required on the machine before starting again.

The tire that had been plugged with rubber bands weeks before in Indiana was now leaking, the air creeping through the fabric and oozing out at several places. The leak was not bad, just about enough to require pumping every day.

The extra tire that had been following along was taken out of the express office and put on. It was a tire that had been punctured and repaired at the factory. It looked all right, but as it turned out the repair was poorly made, and it would have been better to leave on the old tire, inflating it each day.

A small needle-valve was worn so that it leaked; that was replaced. A stiffer spring was inserted in the intake-valve so it would not open quite so easily. A number of minor things were done, and every nut and bolt tried and tightened.

CHAPTER 14

Lexington and Concord

"THE WAYSIDE INN"

Saturday morning, September 7, at eleven o'clock, we left the Touraine for Auburndale, where we lunched, then to Waltham, and from there due north by what is known as Waltham Street to Lexington, striking Massachusetts Avenue just opposite the town hall.

Along this historic highway rode Paul Revere; at his heels followed the regulars of King George. Tablets, stones, and monuments mark every known point of interest from East Lexington to Concord.

In Boston, at the head of Hull Street, Christ Church, the oldest church in the city, still stands, and bears a tablet claiming for its steeple the credit of the signals for Paul Revere; but the Old North Church in North Square, near which Revere lived and where he attended service, and from the belfry of which the lanterns were really hung, disappeared in the conflict it initiated. In the winter of the siege of Boston the old meeting-house was pulled down by the British soldiers and used for firewood. A fit ending of the ancient edifice which had stood for almost exactly one hundred years, and in which the three Mathers, Increase, Cotton, and Samuel, — father, son, and grandson, — had preached the unctuous doctrine of hell-fire and damnation; teaching so incendiary was bound sooner or later to consume its own habitation.

Revere was not the only messenger of warning. For days the patriots had been anxious concerning the stores of arms and ammunition at Concord, and three days before the night of the 18th Revere himself had warned Hancock and Adams at the Clarke home in Lexington that plans were on foot in the enemies' camp to destroy the stores, whereupon a portion was removed to Sudbury and Groton. Before Revere started on his ride, other messengers had been despatched to alarm the country, but at ten o'clock on the memorable night of the 18th he was sent for and bidden to get ready. He got his riding-boots and surtout from his house in North Square, was ferried across the river, landing on the Charlestown side about eleven o'clock, where he was told the signal-lights had already been displayed in the belfry. The moon was rising as he put spurs to his horse and started for Lexington.

The troops were ahead of him by an hour.

He rode up what is now Main Street as far as the "Neck," then took the old Cambridge road for Somerville.

To escape two British officers who barred his way, he dashed across lots to the main road again and took what is now Broadway. On he went over the hill to Medford, where he aroused the Medford minute-men. Then through West Medford and over the Mystic Bridge to Menotomy, — now Arlington, — where he struck the highway, — now Massachusetts Avenue, — to Lexington. Galloping up to the old Clarke house where Hancock and Adams were sleeping, the patriot on guard cautioned him not to make so much noise.

"Noise! you'll have enough of it before long. The Regulars are coming."

Awakened by the voice, Hancock put his head out of the window and said: "Come in, Revere; we're not afraid of you."

Soon the old house was alight. Revere entered the "living room" by the side door and delivered his message to the startled occupants. Soon they were joined by Dawes, another messenger by another road. After refreshing themselves, Revere and Dawes set off for Concord. On the road Samuel Prescott joined them. When about half-way, four British officers, mounted and fully armed, stopped them. Prescott jumped over the low stone wall, made his escape and alarmed Concord. Dawes was chased by two of the officers until, with rare shrewdness, he dashed up in front of a deserted farm-house and shouted, "Hello, boys! I've got two of them," frightening off his pursuers.

Revere was captured. Without fear or humiliation he told his name and his mission. Frightened by the sound of firing at Lexington, the officers released their prisoner, and he made his way back to Hancock and Adams and accompanied them to what is now the town of Burlington. Hastening back to Lexington for a trunk containing valuable papers, he was present at the battle, — the fulfilment of his warning, the red afterglow of the lights from the belfry of Old North Church.

He lived for forty-odd years to tell the story of his midnight ride, and now he sleeps with Hancock and Adams, the parents of Franklin, Peter Faneuil, and a host of worthy men in the "Granary."

The good people of Massachusetts have done what they could to commemorate the events and obliterate the localities of those great days; they have erected monuments and put up tablets in great numbers; but while marking the spots where events occurred, they have changed the old names of roads and places until contemporary accounts require a glossary for interpretation.

Who would recognize classic Menotomy in the tinsel ring of Arlington? The good old Indian name, the very speaking of which is a pleasure, has given place to the first-class apartments, — steam-heated, electric-lights, hot and cold water, all improvements — in appellations of Arlington and Arlington Heights. A tablet marks the spot where on April 19 "the old men of Menotomy" captured a convoy of British soldiers. Poor old men, once the boast and glory of the place that knew you; but now the passing traveller curiously reads the inscription and wonders "Why were they called the old men 'of Menotomy'?" for there is now no such place.

Massachusetts Avenue—Massachusetts Avenue! there's a name, a great, big, luscious name, a name that savors of brown stone fronts and plush rockers: a name which goes well with the commercial prosperity of Boston. Massachusetts Avenue extends from Dorchester in Boston to Lexington Green; it has absorbed the old Cambridge and the old Lexington roads; the old Long Bridge lives in history, but, rechristened Brighton Bridge, the reader fails to identify it.

Concord remains and Lexington remains, simply because no real estate boom has yet reached them but Bunker Hill, there is a feeling that apartments would rent better if the musty associations of the spot were obliterated by some such name as "Buckingham Heights," or "Commonwealth Crest;" "The Acropolis" has been prayerfully considered by the freemen of the modern Athens; — whatever the decision may be, certain it is the name Bunker Hill is a heavy load for choice corners in the vicinity.

There are a few old names still left in Massachusetts, — Jingleberry Hill and Chillyshally Brook sound as if they once meant something; Spot Pond, named by Governor Winthrop, has not lost its birthright; Powder-Horn Hill records its purchase from the Indians for a hornful of powder — probably damp; Drinkwater River is a good name, — Strong Water Brook by many is considered better. It is well to record these names before they are effaced by the commercialism rampant in the suburbs of Boston.

At the Town Hall in Lexington we turned to the right for East Lexington, and made straight for Follen Church, and the home of Dr. Follen close by, where Emerson preached in 1836 and 1837.

The church was not built until 1839. In January, 1840, the congregation had assembled in their new edifice for the dedication services. They waited for their pastor, who was expected home from a visit to New York, but the Long Island Sound steamer — Lexington, by strange coincidence it was called — had burned and Dr. Follen was among the lost. His home is now the East Lexington Branch of the Public Library.

We climbed the stairs that led to the small upper room where Emerson filled his last regular charge. Small as was the room, it probably more than sufficed for the few people who were sufficiently advanced for his notions of a preacher's mission. He did not believe in the rites the church clung to as indispensable; he did not believe in the use of bread and wine in the Lord's Supper; he did not believe in prayers from the pulpit unless the preacher felt impelled to pray; he did not believe in ritualism or formalism of any kind, — in short, he did not believe in a church, for a church, how-ever broad and liberal, is, after all, an institution, and no one man, how-ever great, can support an institution. A very great soul — and Emerson was a great soul — may carry a following through life and long after death, but that following is not a church, not an institution, not a living orga-nized body, until forms, conventions, and traditions make it so; its vitaliz-ing element may be the soul of its founder, but the framework of the structure, the skeleton, is made up of the more or less rigid conventions which are the results of natural and logical selection.

The ritual of Rome, the service of England, the dry formalism of Calvin-ism, the slender structure of Unitarianism were all equally repugnant to Emerson; he could not stretch himself in their fetters; he was not at ease in any priestly garment. Born a prophet, he could not become a priest. By nature a teacher and preacher, he never could submit to those restrictions which go so far to make preaching effective. He taught the lesson of the ages, but he mistook it for his own. He belonged to humanity, but he detached himself. He was a leader, but would acknowledge no discipline. Men cried out to him, but he wandered apart. He was an intellectual anarchist of rare and lovely type; few sweeter souls ever lived, but he defied order.

Not that Emerson would have been any better if he had submitted to the discipline of some church; he did what he felt impelled to do, and left the world a precious legacy of ideas, of brilliant, beautiful thoughts; but thoughts which are brilliant and beautiful as the stars are, scattered jewels against the background of night with no visible connection. Is it not possible that the gracious discipline of an environment more conventional might have reduced these thoughts to some sort of order, brought the stars into constellations, and left suggestions for the ordering of life that would be of greater force and more permanent value?

His wife relates that one day he was reading an old sermon in the little room in the Follen mansion, when he stopped, and said, "The passage which I have just read I do not believe, but it was wrongly placed."

The circumstance illustrates the openness and frankness of his mind, but it is also a commentary on the want of system in his intellectual processes. His habit through life was to jot down thoughts as they came to him; he kept note-books and journals all his life; he dreamed in the pine woods by day and walked beneath the stars by night; he sat by the still waters and wandered in the green fields; and the dreams and the visions and the fancies of the moment he faithfully recorded. These disjointed musings and disconnected thoughts formed the raw material of all he ever said and wrote. From the accumulated stores of years he would draw whatever was necessary to meet the needs of the hour; and it did not matter to him if thought did not dovetail into thought with all the precision of good intellectual carpentry. His edifices were filled with chinks and unfinished apartments.

He saw things in a big way, but did not always see them as through crystal, clearly; nor did he always take his staff in hand and courageously go about to see all sides of things. He never thought to a finish. His philosophy never acquired form and substance. His thoughts are not linked in chain, but are just so many precious pearls lightly strung on a silken thread.

In 1852 he wrote in his journal, "I waked last night and bemoaned myself because I had not thrown myself into this deplorable question of slavery, which seems to want nothing so much as a few assured voices. But then in hours of sanity I recover myself, and say, 'God must govern his own world, and knows his way out of this pit without my desertion of my post, which has none to guard it but me. I have quite other slaves to free than those negroes, to wit, imprisoned spirits, imprisoned thoughts, far back in the brain of man, far retired in the heaven of invention, and which, important to the republic of man, have no watchman or lover or defender but me,'" thereby naïvely leaving to God the lesser task.

But he wrongs himself in his own journal, for he did bestir himself and he did speak, and he did not leave the black men to God while he looked after the white; he helped God all he could in his own peculiar, irresolute way. At the same time no passage from the journals throws more light on the pure soul of the great dreamer. He was opposed to slavery and he felt for the negroes, but their physical degradation did not appeal to him so much as the intellectual degradation of those about him. To him it was a loftier mission to release the minds of men than free their bodies. With the naïve and at the same time superb egoism which is characteristic of great souls, he consoles himself with the thought that God can probably take care of the slavery question without troubling him; he will stick to his post and look after more important matters.

What a treat it must have been to those assembled in the Follen house to hear week after week the very noblest considerations and suggestions concerning life poured forth in tones so musical, so penetrating, that today they ring in the ears of those who had the great good fortune to hear. There was probably very little said about death. Emerson never pretended to a vision beyond the grave. In his essay on "Immortality" he says, "Sixty years ago, the books read, the services and prayers heard, the habits of thought of religious persons, were all directed on death. All were under the shadow of Calvinism and of the Roman Catholic purgatory, and death was dreadful. The emphasis of all the good books given to young people was on death. We were all taught that we were born to die; and over that, all the terrors that theology could gather from savage nations were added to increase the gloom, A great change has occurred. Death is seen as a natural event, and is met with firmness. A wise man in our time caused to be written on his tomb, 'Think on Living.' That inscription describes a progress in opinion. Cease from this antedating of your experience. Sufficient to today are the duties of today. Don't waste life in doubts and fears; spend yourself on the work before you, well assured that the right performance of the hour's duties will be the best preparation for the hours or ages that follow it."

Such was the burden of Emerson's message: make the very best of life; let not the present be palsied by fears for the future. A healthy, sane message, a loud, clear voice in the wilderness of doubt and fears, the very loudest and clearest voice in matters spiritual and intellectual which America has yet produced.

It was during the days of his service in East Lexington that he went to Providence to deliver a course of lectures; while there he was invited to conduct the services in the Second (Unitarian) Church. The pastor said afterwards: "He selected from Greenwood's collection hymns of a purely meditative character, without any distinctively Christian expression. For the Scripture lesson he read a fine passage from Ecclesiasticus, from which he also took his text. The sermon was precisely like one of his lectures in style; the prayers, or what took their place, were wholly without supplication, confession, or praise, but only sweet meditations on nature, beauty, order, goodness, love. After returning home I found Emerson with his head bowed on his hands, which were resting on his knees. He looked up to me and said, 'Now, tell me honestly, plainly, just what you think of that service.' I replied that before he was half through I had made up my mind that it was the last time he should have that pulpit. 'You are right,' he rejoined, 'and I thank you. On my part, before I was half through, I felt out of place. The doubt is solved.'"

He dwelt with time and eternity on a footing of familiar equality. He did not shrink or cringe. His prayers were sweet meditations and his sermon a lecture. He was the apostle of beauty, goodness, and truth.

Lexington Road from East Lexington to the Centre is a succession of historic spots marked by stones and tablets.

The old home of Harrington, the last survivor of the battle of Lexington, still stands close to the roadside, shaded by a row of fine big trees. Harrington died in 1854 at the great age of ninety-eight; he was a fifer-boy in Captain Parker's company. In the early morning on the day of the fight his mother rapped on his bedroom door, calling, "Jonathan, Jonathan, get up; the British are coming, and something must be done." He got up and did his part with the others. Men still living recall the old man; they heard the story of that memorable day from the lips of one who participated therein.

At the corner of Maple Street there is an elm planted in 1740. On a little knoll at the left is the Monroe Tavern. The square, two-storied frame structure which remains is the older portion of the inn as it was in those days. It was the head-quarters of Lord Percy; and it is said that an inoffensive old man who served the soldiers with liquor in the small barroom was killed when he tried to get away by a rear door. When the soldiers left they sacked the house, piled up the furniture and set fire to it. Washington dined in the dining-room in the second story, November 5, 1789. The house was built in 1695, and is still owned by a direct descendant of the first William Monroe.

Not far from the tavern and on the same side of the street is a house where a wounded soldier was cared for by a Mrs. Sanderson, who lived to be one hundred and four years old.

Near the intersection of Woburn Street is a crude stone cannon which marks the place where Lord Percy planted a field pine pointing in the direction of the Green to check the advancing patriots and cover the retreat of the Regulars.

On the triangular "Common," in the very heart of the village, a flat-faced boulder marks the line where the minute-men under Captain Parker were formed to receive the Regulars. "Stand your ground; don't fire unless fired upon; but if they mean to have a war. let it begin here" was Parker's command to his men and it was there the war did begin. The small band of patriots were not yet in line when the red-coats appeared at the east end of the meeting-house, coming on the double-quick.

Riding ahead, a British officer called out, "Disperse, you rebels! Villains, disperse!" but the little band of rebels stood their ground until a fatal volley killed eight and wounded ten. Only two of the British were wounded.

The victors remained in possession of the Green, fired a volley, and gave three loud cheers to celebrate a victory that in the end was to cost King George his fairest colonies.

The soldiers' monument that stands on the Green was erected in 1799. In 1835, in the presence of Daniel Webster, Joseph Story, Josiah Quincy, and a vast audience, Edward Everett delivered an oration, and the bodies of those who fell in the battle were removed from the old cemetery to a vault in the rear of the shaft, where they now rest. The weather-beaten stone is over-grown with a protecting mantle of ivy, which threatens to drop like a veil over the long inscription. Here, for more than a century, the village has received distinguished visitors, — Lafayette in 1824, Kossuth in 1851, and famous men of later days.

The Buckman Tavern, where the patriots assembled, built in 1690, still stands with its marks of bullets and flood of old associations.

These ancient hostelries — Monroe's, Buckman's, Wright's in Concord, and the Wayside Inn — are by no means the least interesting features of this historic section. An old tavern is as pathetic as an old hat: it is redolent of former owners and guests, each room reeks with confused personalities, every latch is electric from many hands, every wall echoes a thousand voices; at dusk of day the clink of glasses and the resounding toast may still be heard in the deserted banquet-hall; at night a ghostly light illumines the vacant ballroom, and the rustle of silks and satins, the sound of merry laughter, and the faint far-off strains of music fall upon the ear.

We did not visit the Clarke house where Paul Revere roused Adams and Hancock; we saw it from the road. Originally, and until 1896, the house stood on the opposite side of the street; the owner was about to demolish it to subdivide the land, when the Historical Society intervened and purchased it.

Neither did we enter the old burying-ground on Elm Street. The automobile is no respecter of persons or places; it pants with impatience if brought to a stand for so much as a moment before a house or monument of interest, and somehow the throbbing, puffing, impatient machine gets the upper hand of those who are supposed to control it; we are hastened onward in spite of our better inclinations.

The trolley line from Lexington to Concord is by way of Bedford, but the direct road over the hill is the one the British followed. It is nine miles by Bedford and the Old Bedford Road, and but six miles direct.

A short distance out of Lexington a tablet marks an old well; the inscription reads, "At this well, April 19, 1775, James Hayward, of Acton, met a British soldier, who, raising his gun, said, 'You are a dead man.' 'And so are you,' replied Hayward. Both fired. The soldier was instantly killed and Hayward mortally wounded."

Grim meeting of two thirsty souls; they sought water and found blood; they wooed life and won death. War is epitomized in the exclamations, "You are a dead man," "And so are you." Further debate would end the strife; the one query, "Why?" would bring each musket to a rest. Poor unknown Britisher, exiled from home, what did he know about the merits of the controversy? What did he care? It was his business to shoot, and be shot. He fulfilled most completely in the same moment the double mission of the soldier, to kill and be killed. Those who do the fighting never do know very much about what they are fighting for, — if they did, most of them would not fight at all. In these days of common schools and newspapers it becomes ever more and more difficult to recruit armies with men who neither know nor think; the common soldier is beginning to have opinions; by and by he will not fight unless convinced he is right, — then there will be fewer wars.

Over the road we were following the British marched in order and retreated in disorder. The undisciplined minute-men were not very good at standing up in an open square and awaiting the onslaught of a company of regulars, — it takes regulars to meet regulars out in the open; but behind trees and fences, from breast-works and scattered points of advantage, each minute-man was a whole army in himself, and the regulars had a hard time of it on their retreat, — the trees and stones which a few hours before had been just trees and stones, became miniature fortresses.

The old vineyard, where in 1855 Ephraim Bull produced the now well known Concord grape by using the native wild grape in a cross with a cultivated variety, is at the outskirts of Concord.

A little farther on is "The Wayside," so named by Hawthorne, who purchased the place from Alcott in 1852, lived there until his appointment as Consul at Liverpool in 1853, and again on his return from England in 1860, until he died in 1864. But "The Wayside" was not Hawthorne's first Concord home. He came there with his bride in 1842 and lived four years in the Old Manse.

There has never been written but one adequate description of this venerable dwelling, and that by Hawthorne himself in "Mosses from an Old Manse." To most readers the description seems part and parcel of the fanciful tales that follow; no more real than the "House of the Seven Gables." We of the outside world who know our Concord only by hearsay cannot realize that "The Wayside" and the "Old Manse" and "Sleepy Hollow" are verities, — verities which the plodding language of prose tails to compass, unless the pen is wielded by a master hand.

Cut in a window-pane of one of the rooms were left these inscriptions: "Nat'l Hawthorne. This is his study, 1843." "Inscribed by my husband at sunset, April 3d, 1843, in the gold light, S. A. H. Man's accidents are God's purposes. Sophia A. Hawthorne, 1843."

Dear, devoted bride, after more than fifty years your bright, loving letters have come to light, and through your clear vision we catch unobstructed glimpses of men and things of those days. After years of devotion to your husband and his memory it was your lot to die and be buried in a foreign land, while he lies lonely in "Sleepy Hollow."

When the honeymoon was still a silver crescent in the sky she wrote a friend, "I hoped I should see you again before I came home to our paradise. I intended to give you a concise history of my Elysian life. Soon after we returned my dear lord began to write in earnest, and then commenced my leisure, because, till we meet at dinner, I do not see him. We were interrupted by no one, except a short call now and then from

Elizabeth Hoar, who can hardly be called an earthly inhabitant; and Mr. Emerson, whose face pictured the promised land (which we were then enjoying), and intruded no more than a sunset or a rich warble from a bird.

"One evening, two days after our arrival at the Old Manse, George Hilliard and Henry Cleveland appeared for fifteen minutes on their way to Niagara Falls, and were thrown into raptures by the embowering flowers and the dear old house they adorned, and the pictures of Holy Mothers mild on the walls, and Mr. Hawthorne's study, and the noble avenue. We forgive them for their appearance here, because they were gone as soon as they had come, and we felt very hospitable. We wandered down to our sweet, sleepy river, and it was so silent all around us and so solitary, that we seemed the only persons living. We sat beneath our stately trees, and felt as if we were the rightful inheritors of the old abbey, which had descended to us from a long line. The tree-tops waved a majestic welcome, and rustled their thousand leaves like brooks over our heads. But the bloom and fragrance of nature had become secondary to us, though we were lovers of it. In my husband's face and eyes I saw a fairer world, of which the other was a faint copy."

Nearly two weeks later she continues in the same letter, "Sweet, dear Mary, nearly a fortnight has passed since I wrote the above. I really believe I will finish my letter today, though I do not promise. That magician upstairs is very potent! In the afternoon and evening I sit in the study with him. It is the pleasantest niche in our temple. We watch the sun, together, descending in purple and gold, in every variety of magnificence, over the river. Lately, we go on the river, which is now frozen; my lord to skate, and I to run and slide, during the dolphin death of day. I consider my husband a rare sight, gliding over the icy stream. For, wrapped in his cloak, he looks very graceful; impetuously darting from me in long, sweeping curves, and returning again — again to shoot away. Our meadow at the bottom of the orchard is like a small frozen sea now; and that is the present scene of our heroic games. Sometimes, in the splendor of the dying light, we seem sporting upon transparent gold, so prismatic becomes the ice; and the snow takes opaline hues from the gems that float above as clouds. It is eminently the hour to see objects, just after the sun has disappeared. Oh, such oxygen as we inhale! After other skaters appear, — young men and boys, — who principally interest me as foils to my husband, who, in the presence of nature, loses all shyness and moves regally like a king. One afternoon Mr. Emerson and Mr. Thoreau went with him down the river. Henry Thoreau is an experienced skater, and was figuring dithyrambic dances and Bacchic leaps on the ice, — very remarkable, but very ugly methought. Next him followed Mr. Hawthorne, who, wrapped in his cloak, moved like a self-impelled Greek statue, stately and grave. Mr. Emerson closed the line, evidently too weary to hold himself erect, pitching headforemost, half lying on the air. He came in to rest himself, and said to me that Hawthorne was a tiger, a bear, a lion, — in short, a satyr, and there was no tiring him out; and he might be the death of a man like himself. And then, turning upon me that kindling smile for which he is so memorable, he added, 'Mr. Hawthorne is such an Ajax, who can cope with him!'"

Of all the pages, ay, of all the books, that have been printed concerning Emerson, Hawthorne, and Thoreau, there is not one which more vividly and accurately set the men before us and describe their essential characteristics than the casual lines of this old letter: — Thoreau, the devotee of nature, "figuring dithyrambic dances and Bacchic leaps on the ice," joyous in the presence of his god; the mystic Hawthorne, wrapped in his sombre cloak, "moved like a self-impelled Greek statue, stately and grave," — with magic force these words throw upon the screen of the imagination the figure of the creator of Hester Prynne and Arthur Dimmesdale; while Emerson is drawn with the inspiration of a poet, "evidently too weary to hold himself erect, pitching headforemost, half lying on the air;" "half lying on the air," — the phrase rings in the ear, lingers in the memory, attaches itself to Emerson, and fits like a garment of soft and yielding texture.

The letter concludes as follows: "After the first snowstorm, before it was so deep, we walked in the woods, very beautiful in winter, and found slides in Sleepy Hollow, where we became children, and enjoyed ourselves as of old, — only more, a great deal. Sometimes it is before breakfast that Mr. Hawthorne goes to skate upon the meadow. Yesterday, before he went out, he said it was very cloudy and gloomy, and he thought it would storm. In half an hour, oh, wonder! what a scene! Instead of a black sky, the rising sun, not yet above the hill, had changed the firmament into a vast rose! On every side, east, west, north, and south, every point blushed roses. I ran to the study and the meadow sea also was a rose, the reflection of that above. And there was my husband, careering about, glorified by the light. Such is Paradise.

"In the evening we are gathered together beneath our luminous star in the study, for we have a large hanging astral lamp, which beautifully illumines the room, with its walls of pale yellow paper, its Holy Mother over the fireplace, and pleasant books, and its pretty bronze vase on one of the secretaries, filled with ferns. Except once, Mr. Emerson, no one hunts us out in the evening. Then Mr. Hawthorne reads to me. At present we can only get along with the old English writers, and we find that they are the hive from which all modern honey is stolen. They are thick-set with thought, instead of one thought serving for a whole book. Shakespeare is pre-eminent; Spencer is music. We dare to dislike Milton when he goes to heaven. We do not recognize God in his picture of Him. There is something so penetrating and clear in Mr. Hawthorne's intellect, that now I am acquainted with it, merely thinking of him as I read winnows the chaff from the wheat at once. And when he reads to me, it is the acutest criticism. Such a voice, too, — such sweet thunder! Whatever is not worth much shows sadly, coming through such a medium, fit only for noblest ideas. From reading his books you can have some idea of what it is to dwell with Mr. Hawthorne. But only a shadow of him is found in his books. The half is not told there."

Just a letter, the outpouring of a loving young heart, written with no thought of print and strange eye, slumbering for more than fifty years to come to light at last; just one of many, all of them well worth reading.

The three great men of Concord were happy in their wives. Mrs. Hawthorne and Mrs. Alcott were not only great wives and mothers, but they could express their prayers, meditations, fancies, and emotions in clear and exquisite English.

It was after the prosperous days of the Liverpool Consulate that Hawthorne returned to Concord to spend the remainder of his all too short life.

He made many changes in "The Wayside" and surrounding grounds. He enlarged the house and added the striking but quite unpicturesque tower which rises from the centre of the main part; here he had his study and point of observation; he could see the unwelcome visitor while yet a far way off, or contemplate the lazy travel of a summer's day.

Just beyond is "Orchard House," into which the Alcotts moved in October, 1858.

A philosopher may not be a good neighbor, and Alcott lived just a little too near Hawthorne. "It was never so well understood at 'The Wayside' that its owner had retiring habits as when Alcott was reported to be approaching along Larch Path, which stretched in feathery bowers between our house and his. Yet I was not aware that the seer failed at any hour to gain admittance, — one cause, perhaps, of the awe in which his visits were held. I remember that my observation was attracted to him curiously from the fact that my mother's eyes changed to a darker gray at his advents, as they did only when she was silently sacrificing herself. I clearly understood that Mr. Alcott was admirable, but he sometimes brought manuscript poetry with him, the dear child of his own Muse. There was one particularly long poem which he had read aloud to my mother and father; a seemingly harmless thing, from which they never recovered."

The appreciation the great men of Concord had of one another is interesting to the outside world. Great souls are seldom congenial, — popular impression to the contrary notwithstanding. Minds of a feather flock together; but minds of gold are apt to remain apart, each sufficient unto itself. It is in sports, pastimes, business, politics, that men congregate with facility; in literary and intellectual pursuits the leaders are anti-pathetic in proportion to their true greatness. Now and then two, and more rarely three, are united by bonds of quick understanding and sympathy, but men of profound convictions attract followers and repel companions.

Emerson's was the most catholic spirit; he understood his neighbors better than they understood one another; his vision was very clear. For a man who mingled so little with the world, who spent so much of his life in contemplation—in communing with his inner self—Emerson was very sane indeed; his idiosyncrasies did not prevent his judging men and things quite correctly.

Hawthorne and Emerson saw comparatively little of each other; these two great souls respected the independence of each other too much to intrude. "Mr. Hawthorne once broke through his hermit usage, and honored Miss Ellen Emerson, the friend of his daughter Una, with a formal call on a Sunday evening. It was the only time, I think, that he ever came to the house except when persuaded to come in for a few moments on the rare occasions when he walked with my father. On this occasion he did not ask for either Mr. or Mrs. Emerson, but announced that his call was upon Miss Ellen. Unfortunately, she had gone to bed, but he remained for a time talking with my sister Edith and me, the school-mates of his children. To cover his shyness he took up a stereoscope on the centre-table and began to look at the pictures. After looking at them for a time he asked where those views were taken. We told him they were pictures of the Concord Court and Town Houses, the Common and the Mill-dam; on hearing which he expressed some surprise and interest, but evidently was as unfamiliar with the centre of the village where he had lived for years as a deer or a wood-thrush would be. He walked through it often on his way to the cars, but was too shy or too rapt to know what was there."

Emerson liked Hawthorne better than his books, — the latter were too weird, uncanny, and inconclusive. In 1838 he noted in his journal, "Elizabeth Peabody brought me yesterday Hawthorne's 'Footprints on the Seashore' to read. I complained there was no inside to it. Alcott and he together would make a man."

Later, when Hawthorne came to live in Concord, Emerson did his best to get better acquainted; but it was of little use; they had too little in common. Both men were great walkers, and yet they seldom walked together. They went to Harvard to see the Shakers, and Emerson recorded it as a "satisfactory tramp; we had good talk on the way."

After Hawthorne's death, Emerson made the following entry in his journal: "I thought him a greater man than any of his works betray; there was still a great deal of work in him, and he might one day show a purer power. It would have been a happiness, doubtless, to both of us, to come into habits of unreserved intercourse. It was easy to talk with him; there were no barriers; only he said so little that I talked too much, and stopped only because, as he gave no indication, I feared to exceed. He showed no egotism or self-assertion; rather a humility, and at one time a fear that he had written himself out. I do not think any of his books worthy his genius. I admired the man, who was simple, amiable, truth-loving, and frank in conversation, but I never read his books with pleasure; they are too young."

Emerson was greedy for ideas, and the pure, limpid literature of Hawthorne did not satisfy him.

Hawthorne's estimate of Emerson was far more just and penetrating; he described him very correctly as "a great original thinker" whose "mind acted upon other minds of a certain constitution with wonderful magnetism, and drew many men upon long pilgrimages to speak with him face to face. Young visionaries — to whom just so much of insight had been imparted as to make life all a labyrinth around them — came to seek the clew that should guide them out of their self-involved bewilderment.

Gray-headed theorists—whose systems, at first air, had finally imprisoned them in an iron framework—travelled painfully to his door, not to ask deliverance, but to invite the free spirit into their own thraldom. People that had lighted on a new thought, or a thought that they fancied new, came to Emerson, as the finder of a glittering gem hastens to a lapidary to ascertain its quality and value. Uncertain, troubled, earnest wanderers through the midnight of the moral world beheld his intellectual face as a beacon burning on a hill-top, and, climbing the difficult ascent, looked forth into the surrounding obscurity more hopefully than hitherto. For myself, there had been epochs in my life when I, too, might have asked of this prophet the master word that should solve me the riddle of the universe, but, now, being happy, I feel as if there were no question to be put, and therefore admired Emerson as a poet of deep and austere beauty, but sought nothing from him as a philosopher. It was good nevertheless to meet him in the wood-paths, or sometimes in our avenue, with that pure, intellectual gleam diffused about his presence like the garment of a shining one; and he, so quiet, so simple, so without pretension, encountering each man alive as if expecting to receive more than he could impart."

It was fortunate for Hawthorne, doubly fortunate for us who read him, that he could withstand the influence of Emerson, and could go on writing in his own way; his dreams and fancies were undisturbed by the clear vision which sought so earnestly to distract him from his realm of the imagination.

On first impressions Emerson rated Alcott very high. "He has more of the godlike than any man I have ever seen, and his presence rebukes, and threatens, and raises. He *is* a teacher." "Yesterday Alcott left us after a three days' visit. The most extraordinary man, and the highest genius of his time." This was in 1835. Seven years later Emerson records this impression. "He looks at everything in larger angles than any other, and, by good right, should be the greatest man. But here comes in another trait; it is found, though his angles are of so generous contents, the lines do not meet; the apex is not quite defined. We must allow for the refraction of the lens, but it is the best instrument I have ever met with."

Alcott visited Concord first in October, 1835, and found that he and Emerson had many things in common, but he entered in his diary, "Mr. Emerson's fine literary taste is sometimes in the way of a clear and hearty acceptance of the spiritual." Again, he naively congratulates himself that he has found a man who could appreciate his theories. "Emerson sees me, knows me, and, more than all others, helps me, — not by noisy praise, not by low appeals to interest and passion, but by turning the eye of others to my stand in reason and the nature of things. Only men of like vision can apprehend and counsel each other."

With the exception of Hawthorne, there was among the men of Concord a tendency to overestimate one another. For the most part, they took themselves and each other very seriously; even Emerson's subtle sense of humor did not save him from yielding to this tendency, which is illustrated in the following page from Hawthorne's journal:

"About nine o'clock (Sunday) Hilliard and I set out on a walk to Walden Pond, calling by the way at Mr. Emerson's to obtain his guidance or directions. He, from a scruple of his eternal conscience, detained us until after the people had got into church, and then he accompanied us in his own illustrious person. We turned aside a little from our way to visit Mr. Hosmer, a yeoman, of whose homely and self-acquired wisdom Mr. Emerson has a very high opinion." "He had a fine flow of talk, and not much diffidence about his own opinions. I was not impressed with any remarkable originality in his views, but they were sensible and characteristic. Methought, however, the good yeoman was not quite so natural as he may have been at an earlier period. The simplicity of his character has probably suffered by his detecting the impression he makes on those around him. There is a circle, I suppose, who look up to him as an oracle, and so he inevitably assumes the oracular manner, and speaks as if truth and wisdom were attiring themselves by his voice. Mr. Emerson has risked the doing him much mischief by putting him in print, — a trial few persons can sustain without losing their unconsciousness. But, after all, a man gifted with thought and expression, whatever his rank in life and his mode of uttering himself, whether by pen or tongue, cannot be expected to go through the world without finding himself out; and, as all such discoveries are partial and imperfect, they do more harm than good to the character. Mr. Hosmer is more natural than ninety-nine men out of a hundred, and is certainly a man of intellectual and moral substance. It would be amusing to draw a parallel between him and his admirer, — Mr. Emerson, the mystic, stretching his hand out of cloudland in vain search for something real; and the man of sturdy sense, all whose ideas seem to be dug out of his mind, hard and substantial, as he digs his potatoes, carrots, beets, and turnips out of the earth. Mr. Emerson is a great searcher for facts, but they seem to melt away and become unsubstantial in his grasp."

They took that extraordinary creature, Margaret Fuller, seriously, and they took a vast deal of poor poetry seriously. Because a few could write, nearly everyone in the village seemed to think he or she could write, and write they did to the extent of a small library most religiously shelved and worshipped in its own compartment in the town library.

Genius is egotism; the superb confidence of these men, each in the sanctity of his own mission, in the plenitude of his own powers, in the inspiration of his own message, made them what they were. The last word was Alcott's because he outlived them all, and his last word was that, great as were those who had taken their departure, the greatest of them all had fallen just short of appreciating him, the survivor. A man penetrates everyone's disguise but his own; we deceive no one but ourselves. The insane are often singularly quick to penetrate the delusions of others; the man who calls himself George Washington ridicules the claim of another that he is Julius Caesar.

Between Hawthorne and Thoreau there was little in common. In 1860, the latter speaks of meeting Hawthorne shortly after his return from Europe, and says, "He is as simple and childlike as ever."

Of Thoreau, Mrs. Hawthorne wrote in a letter, "This evening Mr. Thoreau is going to lecture, and will stay with us. His lecture before was so enchanting; such a revelation of nature in all its exquisite details of wood-thrushes, squirrels, sunshine, mists and shadows, fresh vernal odors, pine-tree ocean melodies, that my ear rang with music, and I seemed to have been wandering through copse and dingle! Mr. Thoreau has risen above all his arrogance of manner, and is as gentle, simple, ruddy, and meek as all geniuses should be; and now his great blue eyes fairly outshine and put into shade a nose which I thought must make him uncomely forever."

In his own journal Hawthorne said, "Mr. Thoreau dined with us. He is a singular character,—a young man with much of wild, original nature still remaining in him; and so far as he is sophisticated, it is in a way and method of his own. He is as ugly as sin, long-nosed, queer-mouthed, and with uncouth and somewhat rustic, though courteous manners, corresponding very well with such an exterior. But his ugliness is of an honest and agreeable fashion, and becomes him much better than beauty."

Alcott helped build the hut at Walden, and he and Emerson spent many an evening there in conversation that must have delighted the gods — in so far as they understood it.

Of Alcott and their winter evenings, Thoreau has said, "One of the last of the philosophers. Connecticut gave him to the world, — he peddled first his wares, afterwards, as he declares, his brains; these he peddles still, prompting God and disgracing man, bearing for fruit his brain only, like the nut in the kernel. His words and attitude always suppose a better state of things than other men are acquainted with, and he will be the last man to be disappointed as the ages revolve. A true friend of man, almost the only friend of human progress. He is perhaps the sanest man and has the fewest crotchets of any I chance to know, — the same yesterday, today, and tomorrow. Ah, such discourse as we had, hermit and philosopher, and the old settler I have spoken of, — we three; it expanded and racked my little home;" — to say nothing of the universe, which doubtless felt the strain.

Referring to the same evening, Alcott said, — probably after a chastening discussion, — "If I were to proffer my earnest prayer to the gods for the greatest of all human privileges, it should be for the gift of a severely candid friend. Intercourse of this kind I have found possible with my friends Emerson and Thoreau; and the evenings passed in their society during these winter months have realized my conception of what friendship, when great and genuine, owes to and takes from its objects."

Nearly twenty years after Thoreau's death, Alcott, while walking towards the close of day, said, "I always think of Thoreau when I look at a sunset."

Emerson was fourteen years older than Thoreau, but between the two men there existed through life profound sympathy and affection. Emerson watched him develop as a young man, and delivered the address at his funeral; for two years they lived in the same house, and concerning him Emerson wrote in 1863, a year after his death, "In reading Henry Thoreau's journal, I am very sensible of the vigor of his constitution. That oaken strength which I noted whenever he walked or worked, or surveyed wood-lots, the same unhesitating hand with which a field laborer accosts a piece of work which I should shun as a waste of strength, Henry shows in his literary task. He has muscle, and ventures in and performs feats which I am forced to decline. In reading him I find the same thoughts, the same spirit that is in me, but he takes a step beyond and illustrates by excellent images that which I should have conveyed in a sleepy generalization. 'Tis as if I went into a gymnasium and saw youths leap and climb and swing with a force unapproachable, tho these feats are only continuations of my initial grapplings and jumps." One is reminded of Mrs. Hawthorne's vivid characterization of the two men as she saw them on the ice of the Musketaquid twenty years before.

In our reverence for a place where a great man for a time has had his home, we must not forget that, while death may mark a given spot, life is quite another matter. A man may be born or may die in a country, a city, a village, a house, a room, or, — narrower still, — a bed; for birth and death are physical events, but life is something quite different. Birth is the welding of the soul to a given body; death is the dissolution of that connection; life is the relation of the imprisoned soul to its environment, and the content of that environment depends largely upon the individual; it may be as narrow as the village in which he lives, or it may stretch beyond the uttermost stars. A man may live on a farm, or he may visit the cities of the earth, — it does not matter much; his life is the sum total of his experiences, his sympathies, his loves, of his hopes and ambitions, his dreams and aspirations, his beliefs and convictions.

To live is to love, and to think, and to dream, and to believe, and to act as one loves and thinks and dreams and believes, that is life; and, therefore, no man's life is bounded by physical confines, no man lives in this place or that, in this house or that; but every man lives in the world he has conquered for himself, and no one knows the limits of the domains of another.

The farmer's boy who sows the seed and watches the tender blades part with volcanic force the surface of the earth, making it to heave and tremble, who sees the buds and flowers of the spring ripen into the fruit and foliage of autumn, who follows with sympathetic vision all the mysterious processes of nature, lives a broader and nobler life than the merchant who sees naught beyond the four walls of his counting-room, or the traveller whose superficial eye marks only the strange and the curious.

In the eyes of those about them Hawthorne "lived" a scant mile from Emerson; in reality they did not live in the same spheres; the boundaries of their worlds did not overlap, but, like two far-separate stars, each felt the distant attraction and admired the glow of the other, and that was all. The real worlds of Thoreau and Alcott and Emerson did at times so far overlap that they trod on common ground, but these periods were so brief and the spaces in common so small that soon they wandered apart, each circling by himself in an orbit of his own.

Words at best are poor instruments of thought; the more we use them the more ambiguous do they become; no man knows exactly what another means from what he says; every word is qualified by its context, but the context of every word is eternity. How long shall we listen to find out what a speaker meant by his opening sentence? — an hour, a day, a week, a month? — these periods are all too short, for with every added thought the meaning of the first is changed for him as well as for us.

"Life" in common speech may mean either mere organic existence or a metaphysical assumption; we speak of the life of a tree, and the life of a man, and the life of a soul, of the life mortal and the life immortal. Who can tell what we have in mind when we talk of life? No one, for we cannot tell ourselves. We speak of life one moment with a certain matter in mind, possibly the state of our garden; in the infinitesimal fraction of a second additional cells of our brain come into activity, additional areas are excited, and our ideas scale the walls of the garden and scatter over the face of the earth. If we attempt to explain, the very process implies the generation of new ideas and the modification of old, so that long before the explanation of what we meant by the use of a given word is finished, the meaning has undergone a change, and we perceive that what we thought we meant by no means included all that lurked in the mind.

In everyday speech we are obliged to distinguish by elaborate circumlocution between a man's place of residence and that larger and truer life, —his sphere of sympathies. Emerson lived in Concord, Carlyle in Chelsea; to the casual reader these phrases convey the impression that the life of Emerson was in some way identified with and bounded by Concord; that the life of Carlyle was in some way identified with and bounded by Chelsea; that in some subtle manner the census of those two small communities affected the philosophy of the two men; whereas we know that for a long time the worlds in which they really did move and have their being so far overlapped that they were near neighbors in thought, much nearer than they would have been if they had "lived" in the same village and met daily on the same streets.

The directory gives a man's abode, but tells us nothing, absolutely nothing, about his life; the number of his house does not indicate where he lives. It is possible to live in London, in Paris, in Rome without ever having visited any one of those places; in truth, millions of people really live in Rome in a truer sense than many who have their abodes there; of the inhabitants of Paris comparatively few really live there, comparatively few have any knowledge of the city, its history, its traditions, its charms, its treasures, but outside Paris there are thousands of men and women who spend many hours and days and weeks of their time in reading, learning, and thinking about Paris and all it contains, — in very truth living there.

Many a worthy preacher lives so exclusively in Jerusalem that he knows not his own country, and his usefulness is impaired; many an artist lives so exclusively in Paris that his work suffers; many an architect lives so long among the buildings of other days that he can do nothing of his own. In fact, most men who are devoted to intellectual, literary, and artistic pursuits live anywhere and everywhere except at home.

The one great merit of Walt Whitman is that he lived in America and in the nineteenth century; he did not live in the past; he did not live in Europe; he lived in the present and in the world about him, his home was America, his era was his own.

If we have no national literature, it is because those who write spend the better part of their lives abroad; they may not leave their own firesides, but all their sympathies are elsewhere, all their inspiration is drawn from other lands and other times.

We have very little art, very little architecture, very little music of our own for the same reasons. We have any number of painters, sculptors, composers, but few of them live at home; their sympathies are elsewhere; they seem to have little or nothing in common with their surroundings. Now and then a clear, fresh voice is heard from out of the woods and fields, or over the city's din, speaking with the convincing eloquence of immediate knowledge and first-hand observation; but there are so few of these voices that they do not amount to a chorus, and a national literature means a chorus.

All this will gradually change until some day the preacher will return from Jerusalem, the painter from Paris, the poet from England, the architect from Rome, and the overwhelming problems presented by the unparalleled development and opportunities of America will absorb their attention to the exclusion of all else.

The danger of travel, the danger of learning, the danger of reading, of profound research and extensive observation, lies in the fact that some age, city, or country, some man or coterie of men, may gain too firm a hold, may so absorb the attention and restrict the imagination that the sense of proportion is lost. It requires a level head to withstand the allurements of the past, the fascination of the foreign. Nothing disturbed

Shakespeare's equanimity. Neither Stratford nor London bounded his life. On the wings of his imagination he visited the known earth and penetrated beyond the blue skies, he made the universe his home; and yet he was essentially and to the last an Englishman.

When we stopped before "Orchard House" it was desolate and forsaken, and the entrance to the "Hillside Chapel," where the "Concord School of Philosophy and Literature" had its home for nine years, was boarded up.

Parts of the house had been built more than a century and a half when Mrs. Alcott bought it in 1857. In her journal for July, 1858, the author of "Little Women" records, "Went into the new house and began to settle. Father is happy; mother glad to be at rest; Anna is in bliss with her gentle John; and May busy over her pictures. I have plans simmering, but must sweep and dust and wash my dishpans a while longer till I see my way."

Meanwhile the little women paper and decorate the walls, May in her enthusiasm filling panels and every vacant place with birds and flowers and mottoes in old English.

"August. Much company to see the new house. All seem to be glad that the wandering family is anchored at last. We won't move again for twenty years" (prophetic soul to name the period so exactly) "if I can help it. The old people need an abiding place, and now that death and love have taken two of us away, I can, I hope, soon manage to take care of the remaining four."

It is one of the ironies of fate that the fame of Bronson Alcott should hang upon that of his gifted daughter. It was not until she made her great success with "Little Women" in 1868 that the outside world began to take a vivid interest in the father. From that time his lectures and conversations began to pay; he was seized anew with the desire to publish, and from 1868 until the beginning of his illness in 1882 he printed or reprinted nearly his entire works, — some eight or ten volumes; it is no disparagement to the kindly old philosopher that his books were bought mainly on the success of his daughter's.

The Summer School of Philosophy was the last ambitious attempt of a spirit that had been struggling for half a century to teach mankind.

The small chapel of plain, unpainted boards, nestling among the trees on the hillside, has not been opened since 1888. It stands a pathetic memento to a vision. Twenty years ago the "school" was an overshadowing reality, — today it is a memory, a minor incident in the progress of thought, a passing phase in intellectual development. Many eminent men lectured there, and the scope of the work is by no means indicated by the humble building which remains; but, while strong in conversation and in the expression of his own views, Alcott was not cut out for a leader. All reports indicate that he had a wonderful facility in the off-hand expression of abstruse thought, but he had no faculty whatsoever for so ordering and systematizing his thoughts as to furnish explosive material for belligerent followers; the intellectual ammunition he put up was not in the convenient form of cartridges, nor even in kegs or barrels, but just poured out on the ground, where it disintegrated before it could be used.

Leaning on the gate that bright, warm, summer afternoon, it was not difficult to picture the venerable, white-haired philosopher seated by the doorstep arguing eloquently with some congenial visitor, or chatting with his daughter. One could almost see a small throng of serious men and women wending their way up the still plainly marked path to the chapel, and catch the measured tones of the lecturer as he expounded theories too recondite for this practical age and generation.

Philosophy is the sarcophagus of truth; and most systems of philosophy are like the pyramids, — impressive piles of useless intellectual masonry, erected at prodigious cost of time and labor to secrete from mankind the truth.

A little farther on we came to the fork in the road where Lincoln Street branches off to the southeast. Emerson's house fronts on Lincoln and is a few rods from the intersection with Lexington Street. Here Emerson lived from 1835 until his death in 1882.

It is singular the fascination exercised by localities and things identified with great men. It is not enough to simply see, but in so far as possible we wish to place ourselves in their places, to walk where they walked, sit where they sat, sleep where they slept, to merge our petty and obscure individualities for the time being in theirs, to lose our insignificant selves in the atmosphere they created and left behind.

Is it possible that subtle distillations of personality penetrate and saturate inanimate things, so that aromas imperceptible to the sense are given off for ages and affect all who come in receptive mood within their influence? It is quite likely that what we feel when we stand within the shadow of a great soul is all subjective, that our emotions are but the workings of our imaginations stirred by suggestive surroundings; but who knows, who knows?

When this house was nearly destroyed by fire in July, 1872, friends persuaded Emerson to go abroad with his daughter, and while they were away, the house was completely restored.

His son describes his return: "When the train reached Concord, the bells were rung and a great company of his neighbors and friends accompanied him, under a triumphal arch, to his restored house. He was greatly moved, but with characteristic modesty insisted that this was a welcome to his daughter, and could not be meant for him. Although he had felt quite unable to make any speech, yet, seeing his friendly townspeople, old and young, in groups watching him enter his own door once more, he turned suddenly back and going to the gate said, 'My friends! I know this is not a tribute to an old man and his daughter returned to their home, but to the common blood of us all — one family — in Concord.'"

The exposure incidental to the fire seriously undermined Emerson's already failing health; shortly after he wrote to a friend in Philadelphia, "It is too ridiculous that a fire should make an old scholar sick; but the exposures of that morning and the necessities of the following days which kept me a large part of the time in the blaze of the sun have in every way demoralized me for the present, — incapable of any sane or just action. These signal proofs of my debility an decay ought to persuade you at your first northern excursion to come and reanimate and renew the failing powers of your still affectionate old friend."

The story of his last days is told by his son, who was also his physician:

"His last few years were quiet and happy. Nature gently drew the veil over his eyes; he went to his study and tried to work, accomplished less and less, but did not notice it. However, he made out to look over and index most of his journals. He enjoyed reading, but found so much difficulty in conversation in associating the right word with his idea, that he avoided going into company, and on that account gradually ceased to attend the meetings of the Social Circle. As his critical sense became dulled, his standard of intellectual performance was less exacting, and this was most fortunate, for he gladly went to any public occasion where he could hear, and nothing would be expected of him. He attended the Lyceum and all occasions of speaking or reading in the Town Hall with unfailing pleasure.

"He read a lecture before his townpeople each winter as late as 1880, but needed to have one of his family near by to help him out with a word and assist in keeping the place in his manuscript. In these last years he liked to go to church. The instinct had always been there, but he had felt that he could use his time to better purpose."

"In April, 1882, a raw and backward spring, he caught cold, and increased it by walking out in the rain and, through forgetfulness, omitting to put on his over-coat. He had a hoarse cold for a few days, and on the morning of April 19 I found him a little feverish, so went to see him next day. He was asleep on his study sofa, and when he awoke he proved to be more feverish and a little bewildered, with unusual difficulty in finding the right word. He was entirely comfortable and enjoyed talking, and, as he liked to have me read to him, I read Paul Revere's Ride, finding that he could only follow simple narrative. He expressed great pleasure, was delighted that the story was part of Concord's story, but was sure he had never heard it before, and could hardly be made to understand who Longfellow was, though he had attended his funeral the week before."

It was at Longfellow's funeral that Emerson got up from his chair, went to the side of the coffin and gazed long and earnestly upon the familiar face of the dead poet; twice he did this, then said to a friend near him, "That gentleman was a sweet, beautiful soul, but I have entirely forgotten his name."

Continuing the narrative, the son says: "Though dulled to other impressions, to one he was fresh as long as he could understand anything, and while even the familiar objects of his study began to look strange, he smiled and pointed to Carlyle's head and said, 'That is my man, my good man!' I mention this because it has been said that this friendship cooled, and that my father had for long years neglected to write to his early friend. He was loyal while life lasted, but had been unable to write a letter for years before he died. Their friendship did not need letters.

"The next day pneumonia developed itself in a portion of one lung and he seemed much sicker; evidently believed he was to die, and with difficulty made out to give a word or two of instructions to his children. He did not know how to be sick, and desired to be dressed and sit up in his study, and as we had found that any attempt to regulate his actions lately was very annoying to him, and he could not be made to understand the reasons for our doing so in his condition, I determined that it would not be worth while to trouble and restrain him as it would a younger person who had more to live for. He had lived free; his life was essentially spent, and in what must almost surely be his last illness we would not embitter the occasion by any restraint that was not absolutely unavoidable.

"He suffered very little, took his nourishment well, but had great annoyance from his inability to find the words which he wished for. He knew his friends and family, but thought he was in a strange house. He sat up in a chair by the fire much of the time, and only on the last day stayed entirely in bed.

"During the sickness he always showed pleasure when his wife sat by his side, and on one of the last days he managed to express, in spite of his difficulty with words, how long and happy they had lived together. The sight of his grandchildren always brought the brightest smile to his face. On the last day he saw several of his friends and took leave of them.

"Only at the last came pain, and this was at once relieved by ether, and in the quiet sleep this produced he gradually faded away in the evening of Thursday, April 27, 1882.

"Thirty-five years earlier he wrote one morning in his journal: 'I said, when I awoke, after some more sleepings and wakings I shall lie on this mattress sick; then dead; and through my gay entry they will carry these bones. Where shall I be then? I lifted my head and beheld the spotless orange light of the morning streaming up from the dark hills into the wide universe.'"

After a few more sleepings and a few more wakings we shall all lie dead, every living soul on this broad earth, — all who, at this mathematical point in time called the present, breathe the breath of life will pass away; but even now the new generation is springing into life; within the next hour five thousand bodies will be born into the world to perpetuate mankind; the whole lives by the constant renewal of its parts; but the individual, what becomes of the individual?

The five thousand bodies that are born within the hour take the place of the something less than five thousand bodies that die within the hour; the succession is preserved; the life of the aggregate is assured; but the individual, what becomes of the individual? Is he immortal, and if immortal whence came he and whither does he go? If immortal, whence come these new souls which are being delivered on the face of the globe at the rate of nearly a hundred a minute? Are they from other worlds, exiled for a time to this, or are they souls revisiting their former habitation? Hardly the latter, for more are coming than going.

One midsummer night, while leaning over the rail of an ocean steamer and watching the white foam thrown up by the prow, the expanse of dark, heaving water, the vast dome of sky studded with the brilliant jewels of space, an old man stopped by my side and we talked of the grandeur of nature and the mysteries of life and death, and he said, "My wife and I once had three boys, whom we loved better than life; one by one they were taken from us, — they all died, and my wife and I were left alone in the world; but after a time a boy was born to us and we gave him the name of the oldest who died, and then another came and we gave him the name of my second boy, and then a third was born and we gave him the name of our youngest; — and so in some mysterious way our three boys have come back to us; we feel that they went away for a little while and returned. I have sometimes looked in their eyes and asked them if anything they saw or heard seemed familiar, whether there was any faint fleeting memories of other days; they say 'no;' but I am sure that their souls are the souls of the boys we lost."

And why not? Is it not more than likely that there is but one soul which dwells in all things animate and inanimate, or rather, are not all things animate and inanimate but manifestations of the one soul, so that the death of an individual is, after all, but the suppression of a particular manifestation and in no sense a release of a separate soul; so that the birth of a child is but a new manifestation in physical form of the one soul, and in no sense the apparition of an additional soul? It is difficult to think otherwise. The birth and death of souls are inconceivable; the immortality of a vast and varying number of individual souls is equally inconceivable. Immortality implies unity, not number. The mind can grasp the possibility of one soul, the manifestation of which is the universe and all it contains.

The hypothesis of individual souls first confined in and then released from individual bodies to preserve their individuality for all time is inconceivable, since it assumes — to coin a word — an intersoulular space, which must necessarily be filled with a medium that is either material or spiritual in its character; if material, then we have the inconceivable condition of spiritual entities surrounded by a material medium; if the intersoulular space be occupied by a spiritual medium, then we have simply souls surrounded by soul, — or, in the final analysis, one soul, of which the so-called individual souls are but so many manifestations.

To the assumption of an all-pervading ether which is the physical basis of the universe, may we not add the suprasumption of an all-pervading soul which is the spiritual basis of not only the ether but of life itself? The seeming duality of mind and matter, of the soul and body, must terminate somewhere, must merge in identity. Whether that identity be the Creator of theology or the soul of speculation does not much matter, since the final result is the same, namely, the immortality of that suprasumption, the soul.

But the individual, what becomes of the individual in this assumption of an all-pervading, immortal soul, of which all things animate and inanimate are but so many activities?

The body, which for a time being is a part of the local manifestation of the pervading soul, dies and is resolved into its constituent elements; it is inconceivable that those elements should ever gather themselves together again and appear in visible, tangible form. No one could possibly desire they ever should; those who die maimed, or from sickness and disease, or in the decrepitude and senility of age, could not possibly wish that their disordered bodies should appear again; nor could any person name the exact period of his life when he was so satisfied with his physical condition that he would choose to have his body as it then was. No; the body, like the trunk of a fallen tree, decays and disappears; like ripe fruit, it drops to the earth and enriches the soil, but nevermore resumes its form and semblance.

The pervading soul, of which the body was but the physical manifestation, remains; it does not return to heaven or any hypothetical point in either space or speculation. The dissolution of the body is but the dissolution of a particular manifestation of the all-pervading soul, and the immortality of the so-called individual soul is but the persistence of that, so to speak, local disturbance in the one soul after the body has disappeared. It is quite conceivable, or rather the reverse is inconceivable, that the activity of the pervading soul, which manifests itself for a time in the body, persists indefinitely after the physical manifestation has ceased; that, with the cessation of the physical manifestation, the particular activity which we recognize here as an individuality will so persist that hereafter we may recognize it as a spiritual personality. In other words, assuming the existence of a soul of which the universe and all it contains are but so many manifestations, it is dimly conceivable that with the cessation, or rather the transformation, of any particular manifestation, the effects may so persist as to be forever known and recognizable, — not by parts of the one soul, which has no parts, but by the soul itself.

Therefore all things are immortal. Nothing is so lost to the infinite soul as to be wholly and totally obliterated. The withering of a flower is as much the act of the all-pervading soul as the death of a child; but the life and death of a human being involve activities of the soul so incomparably greater than the blossoming of a plant, that the immortality of the one, while not differing in kind, may be infinitely more important in degree. The manifestation of the soul in the life of the humming-bird is slight in comparison with the manifestation in the life of a man, and the traces which persist forever in the case of the former are probably insignificant compared with the traces which persist in the case of the latter; but traces must persist, else there is no immortality of the individual; at the same time there is not the slightest reason for urging that, whereas traces of the soul's activity in the form of man will persist, traces of the soul's activity in lower forms of life and in things inanimate will not persist. There is no reason why, when the physical barriers which exist between us and the soul that is within and without us are destroyed, we should not desire to know forever all that the universe contains. Why should not the sun and the moon and the stars be immortal, — as immortal in their way as we in ours, both immortal in the one all-pervading soul?

"The philosophy of six thousand years has not searched the chambers and the magazine of the soul. In its experiments there has always remained, in the last analysis, a residuum it could not solve," said Emerson in the lecture he called "Over-Soul."

What a pity to use the phrase "Over-Soul,' which removes the soul even farther aloof than it is in popular conception, or which fosters the belief of an inner and outer, or an inferior and a superior soul; whereas Emerson meant, as the context shows, the all-pervading soul.

But, then, who knows what anyone else thinks or means? At the most we only know what others say, what words they use, but in what sense they use them and the content of thought back of them we do not know. So far as the problems of life go we are all groping in the dark, and words are like fireflies leading us hither and thither with glimpses of light only to go out, leaving us in darkness and despair.

It is the sounding phrase that catches the ear. "For fools admire and like all things the more which they perceive to be concealed under involved language, and determine things to be true which can prettily tickle the ears and are varnished over with finely sounding phrase," says Lucretius. We imagine we understand when we do not; we do not really, truly, and wholly understand Emerson or any other man; we do not understand ourselves.

We speak of the conceivable and of the inconceivable as if the words had any clear and tangible meaning in our minds; whereas they have not; at the best they are of but relative value. What is conceivable to one man is inconceivable to another; what is beyond the perception of one generation is matter of fact to the next.

The conceivable is and ever must be bounded by the inconceivable; the domain of the former is finite, that of the latter is infinite. It matters not how far we press our speculations, how extravagant our hypotheses, how distant our vision, we reach at length the confines of our thought and admit the inconceivable. The inconceivable is a postulate as essential to reason as is the conceivable. That the inconceivable exists is as certain as the existence of the conceivable; it is in a sense more certain, since we constantly find ourselves in error in our conclusions concerning the existence of the things we know, while we can never be in error concerning the existence of things we can never know, being sure that beyond the confines of the finite there must necessarily be the infinite.

We may indulge in assumptions concerning the infinite based upon our knowledge of the finite, or, rather, based upon the inflexible laws of our mental processes. We may say that there must be one all-pervading soul, not because we can form any conception whatsoever of the true nature of such a soul, but because the alternative hypothesis of many individual souls is utterly obnoxious to our reason.

To those who urge that it is idle to reason about what we cannot conceive, it is sufficient answer to say that man cannot help it. The scientist and the materialist in the ardent pursuit of knowledge soon experience the necessity of indulging in assumptions concerning force and matter, the hypothetical ether and molecules, atoms and vortices, which are as purely metaphysical as any assumptions concerning the soul. The distinction between the realist and the idealist is a matter of temperament. All that separated Huxley from Gladstone was a word; each argued from the unknowable, but disputed over the name and attributes of the inconceivable. Huxley said he did not know, which was equivalent to the dogmatic assertion that he did; Gladstone said he did know, which was a confession of ignorance denser than that of agnosticism.

Those men who try not to think or reason concerning the infinite simply imprison themselves within the four walls of the cell they construct. It is better to think and be wrong than not to think at all. Any assumption is better than no assumption, any belief better than none.

Hypotheses enlarge the boundaries of knowledge. With assumptions the intellectual prospector stakes out the infinite. In life we may not verify our premises, but death is the proof of all things.

We stopped at Wright's tavern, where patriots used to meet before the days of the revolution, and where Major Pitcairn is said — wrongfully in all probability — to have made his boast on the morning of the 19th, as he stirred his toddy, that they would stir the rebels' blood before night.

One realizes that "there is but one Concord" as the carriages of pilgrims are counted in the Square, and the swarm of young guides, with pamphlets and maps, importune the chance visitor.

We chose the most persistent little urchin, not that we could not find our way about so small a village, but because he wanted to ride, and it is always interesting to draw out a child; his story of the town and its famous places was, of course, the one he had learned from the others, but his comments were his own, and the incongruity of going over the sacred ground in an automobile had its effect.

It was a short run down Monument Street to the turn just beyond the "Old Manse." Here the British turned to cross the North Bridge on their way to Colonel Barrett's house, where the ammunition was stored. Just across the narrow bridge the "embattled farmers stood and fired the shot heard round the world." A monument marks the spot where the British received the fire of the farmers, and a stone at the side recites "Graves of two British soldiers," — unknown wanderers from home they surrendered their lives in a quarrel, the merits of which they did not know. "Soon was their warfare ended; a weary night march from Boston, a rattling volley of musketry across the river, and then these many years of rest. In the long procession of slain invaders who passed into eternity from the battle-field of the revolution, these two nameless soldiers led the way." While standing by the grave, Hawthorne was told a story, a tradition of how a youth, hurrying to the battle-field axe in hand, came upon these two soldiers, one not yet dead raised himself up painfully on his hands and knees, and how the youth on the impulse of the moment cleft the wounded man's head with the axe. The tradition is probably false, but it made its impression on Hawthorne, who continues, "I could wish that the grave might be opened; for I would fain know whether either of the skeleton soldiers has the mark of an axe in his skull. The story comes home to me like truth. Oftentimes, as an intellectual and moral exercise, I have sought to follow that poor youth through his subsequent career and observe how his soul was tortured by the blood-stain, contracted as it had been before the long custom of war had robbed human life of its sanctity, and while it still seemed murderous to slay a brother man. This one circumstance has borne more fruit for me than all that history tells us of the fight."

There are souls so callous that the taking of a human life is no more than the killing of a beast; there are souls so sensitive that they will not kill a living thing. The man who can relate without regret so profound it is close akin to remorse the killing of another—no matter what the provocation or the circumstances—is next kin to the common hangman.

From the windows of the "Old Manse," the Rev. William Emerson, grandfather of Ralph Waldo Emerson, looked out upon the battle, and he would have taken part in the fight had not his neighbors held him back; as it was, he sacrificed his life the following year in attempting to join the army at Ticonderoga, contracting a fever which proved fatal.

Sleepy Hollow Cemetery lies on Bedford Street not far from the Town Hall. We followed the winding road to the hill where Hawthorne, Thoreau, the Alcotts, and Emerson lie buried within a half-dozen paces of one another.

Thoreau came first in May, 1862. Emerson delivered the funeral address. Mrs. Hawthorne writes in her diary, "Mr. Thoreau died this morning. The funeral services were in the church. Mr. Emerson spoke. Mr. Alcott read from Mr. Thoreau's writings. The body was in the vestibule covered with wild flowers. We went to the grave."

Hawthorne came next, just two years later. "On the 24th of May, 1864 we carried Hawthorne through the blossoming orchards of Concord," says James T. Fields, "and laid him down under a group of pines, on a hillside, overlooking historic fields. All the way from the village church to the grave the birds kept up a perpetual melody. The sun shone brightly, and the air was sweet and pleasant, as if death had never entered the world. Longfellow and Emerson, Channing and Hoar, Agassiz and Lowell, Greene and Whipple, Alcott and Clarke, Holmes and Hillard, and other friends whom he loved, walked slowly by his side that beautiful spring morning. The companion of his youth and his manhood, for whom he would willingly, at any time, have given up his own life, Franklin Pierce, was there among the rest, and scattered flowers into the grave. The unfinished 'Romance,' which had cost him so much anxiety, the last literary work on which he had ever been engaged, was laid in his coffin."

Eighteen years later, on April 30, 1882, Emerson was laid at rest a little beyond Hawthorne and Thoreau in a spot chosen by himself.

A special train came from Boston, but many could not get inside the church. The town was draped; "even the homes of the very poor bore outward marks of grief." At the house, Dr. Furness, of Philadelphia, conducted the services. "The body lay in the front northeast room, in which were gathered the family and close friends." The only flowers were lilies of the valley, roses, and arbutus.

At the church, Judge Hoar, standing by the coffin, spoke briefly; Dr. Furness read selections from the Scriptures; James Freeman Clarke delivered the funeral address, and Alcott read a sonnet.

"Over an hour was occupied by the passing files of neighbors, friends, and visitors looking for the last time upon the face of the dead poet. The body was robed completely in white, and the face bore a natural and peaceful expression. From the church the procession took its way to the cemetery. The grave was made beneath a tall pine-tree upon the hill-top of Sleepy Hollow, where lie the bodies of his friends Thoreau and Hawthorne, the upturned sod being concealed by strewings of pine boughs. A border of hemlock spray surrounded the grave and completely lined its sides. The services were very brief, and the casket was soon lowered to its final resting-place. The grandchildren passed the open grave and threw flowers into it."

In her "Journal," Louisa Alcott wrote, "Thursday, 27th. Mr. Emerson died at nine P.M. suddenly. Our best and greatest American gone. The nearest and dearest friend father ever had, and the man who has helped me most by his life, his books, his society. I can never tell all he has been to me, — from the time I sang Mignon's song under his window (a little girl) and wrote letters *à la* Bettine to him, my Goethe, at fifteen, up through my hard years, when his essays on Self-Reliance, Character, Compensation, Love, and Friendship helped me to understand myself and life, and God and Nature. Illustrious and beloved friend, good-by!

"Sunday, 30th. — Emerson's funeral. I made a yellow lyre of jonquils for the church, and helped trim it up. Private service at the house, and a great crowd at the church. Father read his sonnet, and Judge Hoar and others spoke. Now he lies in Sleepy Hollow among his brothers under the pines he loved."

On March 4, 1888, Bronson Alcott died, and two days later Louisa Alcott followed her father. They lie near together on the ridge a little beyond Hawthorne. Initials only mark the graves of her sisters, but it has been found necessary to place a small stone bearing the name "Louisa" on the grave of the author of "Little Women." She had made every arrangement for her death, and by her own wish her funeral was in her father's rooms in Boston, and attended by only a few of her family and nearest friends.

"They read her exquisite poem to her mother, her father's noble tribute to her, and spoke of the earnestness and truth of her life. She was remembered as she would have wished to be. Her body was carried to Concord and placed in the beautiful cemetery of Sleepy Hollow, where her dearest ones were already laid to rest. 'Her boys' went beside her as 'a guard of honor,' and stood around as she was placed across the feet of father, mother, and sister, that she might 'take care of them as she had done all her life.'"

Louisa Alcott's last written words were the acknowledgment of the receipt of a flower. "It stands beside me on Marmee's (her mother) worktable, and reminds me tenderly of her favorite flowers; and among those used at her funeral was a spray of this, which lasted for two weeks afterwards, opening bud by bud in the glass on her table, where lay the dear old 'Jos. May' hymn-book, and her diary with the pen shut in as she left it when she last wrote there, three days before the end, 'The twilight is closing about me, and I am going to rest in the arms of my children.' So, you see, I love the delicate flower and enjoy it very much."

Reverently, with bowed heads, we stood on that pine-covered ridge which contained the mortal remains of so many who are great and illustrious in the annals of American literature. A scant patch of earth hides their dust, but their fancies, their imaginings, their philosophy spanned human conduct, emotions, beliefs, and aspirations from the cradle to the grave.

The warm September day was drawing to a close; the red sun was sinking towards the west; the hilltop was aflame with a golden glow from the slanting rays of the declining sun. Slowly we wended our way through the shadowy hollow below; looking back, the mound seemed crowned with glory.

Leaving Concord by Main Street we passed some famous homes, among them Thoreau's earlier home, where he made lead-pencils with the deftness which characterized all his handiwork; turning to the left on Thoreau Street we crossed the tracks and took the Sudbury road through all the Sudburys, — four in number; the roads were good and the country all the more interesting because not yet invaded by the penetrating trolley. It would be sacrilegious for electric cars to go whizzing by the ancient tombs and monuments that fringe the road down through Sudbury; the automobile felt out of place and instinctively slowed down to stately and measured pace.

In all truth, one should walk, not ride, through this beautiful country, where every highway has its historic associations, every burying-ground its honored dead, every hamlet its weather-beaten monument. But if one is to ride, the automobile—incongruous as it may seem—has this advantage,—it will stand indefinitely anywhere; it may be left by the roadside for hours; no one can start it; hardly any person would maliciously harm it, providing it is far enough to one side so as not to frighten passing horses; excursions on foot may be made to any place of interest, then, when the day draws to a close, a half-hour suffices to reach the chosen resting-place.

It was getting dark as we passed beneath the stately trees bordering the old post-road which leads to the door of the "Wayside Inn."

Here the stages from Boston to Worcester used to stop for dinner. Here Washington, Lafayette, Burgoyne, and other great men of Revolutionary days had been entertained, for along this highway the troops marched and countermarched.

The old inn is rich in historic associations.

The road which leads to the very door of the inn is the old post-road; the finely macadamized State road which passes a little farther away is of recent dedication, and is located so as to leave the ancient hostelry a little retired from ordinary travel.

A weather-beaten sign with a red horse rampant swings at one corner of the main building.

"Half effaced by rain and shine, The Red Horse prances on the sign."

For nearly two hundred years, from 1683 to 1860, the inn was owned and kept by one family, the Howes, and was called by many "Howe's Tavern," by others "The Red Horse Inn."

Since the publication of Longfellow's 'Tales of a Wayside Inn," the place has been known by no other name than the one it now bears.

> As ancient is this hostelry
> As any in the land may be,
> Built in the old Colonial day,
> When men lived in a grander way,
> With ampler hospitality;
> A kind of old Hobgoblin Hall,
> Now somewhat fallen to decay,

With weather-stains upon the wall,
And stairways worn, and crazy doors,
And creaking and uneven floors,
And chimneys huge, and tiled and tall.

A portrait of Lyman Howe, the last landlord of the family, hangs in the little barroom,

A man of ancient pedigree,
A Justice of the Peace was he,
Known in all Sudbury as 'The Squire.'
Proud was he of his name and race,
Of old Sir William and Sir Hugh.

And now as of yore

In the parlor, full in view,
His coat-of-arms, well framed and glazed,
Upon the wall in colors blazed.

The small window-panes which the poet describes as bearing—

The jovial rhymes, that still remain,
Writ near a century ago,
By the great Major Molineaux,
Whom Hawthorne has immortal made,

—are preserved in frames near the mantel in the parlor, one deeply scratched by diamond ring with name of Major Molineaux and the date, "June 24th, 1774," the other bears this inscription,—

What do you think?
Here is good drink,
Perhaps you may not know it;
If not in haste, Do stop and taste,
You merry folk will show it.

A worthy, though not so gifted, successor of the jolly major rendered the following "true accomp.," which, yellow and faded, hangs on the barroom wall:

Thursday, August 7th, 1777

		£	s.	d.
	Super & Loging	0	1	4
8th	Brakfast, Dinar and	0	1	9
	Super and half mug of tody	0	2	6
9th	Lodging, one glass rum half	0	2	6
	& Dinar, one mes oats	0	1	4
	Super, half mug flyp	0	3	0
10th	Brakf.-one dram	0	1	8
	Dinner, Lodging, horse-keeping	0	2	0
	one mug flyp, horse bating	0	3	0
11th	horse keeping		1	
13th	glass rum & Diner		1	8
14th	Horse bating	0	0	6
	Horse Jorney 28 miles	0	5	10
	A true accomp-total	1	14	6
	William Bradford.			
	Delivered to Capt. Crosby	2	2	6

Alas! the major's inscription and the foregoing "accomp." are hollow mockeries to the thirsty traveller, for there is neither rum nor "flyp" to be had; the bar is dry as an old cork; the door of the cupboard into which the jovial Howes were wont to stick the awl with which they opened bottles still hangs, worn completely through by the countless jabs, a melancholy reminder of the convivial hours of other days. The restrictions of more abstemious times have relegated the ancient bar to dust, the idle awl to slow-consuming rust.

It is amazing how thirsty one gets in the presence of musty associations of a convivial character. The ghost of a spree is a most alluring fellow; it is the dust on the bottle that flavors the wine; a musty bin is the soul's delight; we drink the vintage and not the wine.

Drinking is a lost art, eating a forgotten ceremony. The pendulum has swung from Trimalchio back to Trimalchio. Quality is lost in quantity. The tables groan, the cooks groan, the guests groan, — feasting is a nightmare.

Wine is a subject, not a beverage; it is discussed, not drunk; it is sipped, tasted, and swallowed reluctantly; it lingers on the palate in fragrant and delicious memory; it comes a bouquet and departs an aroma; it is the fruition of years, the distillation of ages; a liquid jewel, it reflects the subtle colors of the rainbow, running the gamut from a dull red glow to the violet rays that border the invisible.

But, alas! the appreciation of wine is lost. Everybody serves wine, no one understands it; everybody drinks it, no one loves it. From a fragrant essence wine has become a coarse reality, — a convention. Chablis with the oysters, sherry with the soup, sauterne with the fish, claret with the roast, Burgundy with the game, — champagne somewhere, anywhere, everywhere; port, grand, old ruddy port — that has disappeared; no one understands it and no one knows when to serve it; while Madeira, that bloom of the vinous century plant, that rare exotic which ripens with passing generations, is all too subtle for our untutored discrimination.

And if, perchance, a good wine, like a strange guest, finds its way to the table, we are at loss how to receive it, how to address it, how to entertain it. We offend it in the decanting and distress it in the serving. We buy our wines in the morning and serve them in the evening to drink the sediment which the more fastidious wine during long years has been slowly rejecting; we mix the bright transparent liquid with its dregs and our rough palates detect no difference. But the lover of wine, the more he has the less he drinks, until, in the refinement and exaltation of his taste, it is sufficient to look upon the dust-mantled bottle and recall the delicious aroma and flavor, the recollection of which is far too precious to risk by trying anew; he knows that if a bottle be so much as turned in its couch it must sleep again for years before it is really fit to drink; he knows how difficult it is to get the wine out of the bottle clear as ruby or yellow diamond; he knows that if so much as a speck of sediment gets into the decanter, to precisely the extent of the speck is the wine injured.

In serving wines, we of the Western world may learn something from the tea ceremonies of the Japanese, — ceremonies so elaborate that to our impatient notions they are infinitely tedious, and yet they get from the tea all the exquisite delight it contains, and at the same time invest its serving with a halo of form, tradition, and association. Surely, if wine is to be taken at all, it is as precious as a cup of tea; and if taken ceremoniously, it will be taken moderately.

What is the use of serving good wine? No one recognizes it, appreciates it, or cares for it. It is served by the butler and removed by the footman without introduction, greeting, or comment. The Hon. Sam Jones, from Podunk, is announced in stentorian tones as he makes his advent, but the gem of the dinner, the treat of the evening, the flower of the feast, an Haut Brion of '75, or an Yquem of '64, or a Johannisberger of '61, comes in like a tramp without a word.

Possibly one of the guests, whose palate has not been blunted by coarse living or seared by strong drink, may feel that he is drinking something out of the ordinary, and he may linger over his glass, loath to sip the last drop; but all the others gulp their wine, or leave it—with the indifference of ignorance.

Good wine is loquacious; it is a great traveller and smacks of many lands; it is a bon vivant and has dined with the select of the earth; it recalls a thousand anecdotes; it reeks with reminiscences; it harbors a kiss and reflects a glance, but it is a silent companion to those who know it not, and it is quarrelsome with those who abuse it.

It seemed a pity that somewhere about the inn, deep in some long disused cellar, there were not a few — just a few — bottles of old wine, a half-dozen port of 1815, one or two squat bottles of Madeira brought over by men who knew Washington, an Yquem of '48, a Margaux of '58, a Johannisberger Cabinet—not forgetting the "Auslese"—of '61, with a few bottles of Romani Conti and Clos de Vougeot of '69 or '70, — not to exceed two or three dozen all told; not a plebeian among them, each the chosen of its race, and all so well understood that the very serving would carry one back to colonial days, when to offer a guest a glass of Madeira was a subtle tribute to his capacity and appreciation.

It is a far cry from an imaginary banquet with Lucullus to the New England Saturday night supper of pork and beans which was spread before us that evening. The dish is a survival of the rigid Puritanism which was the affliction and at the same time the making of New England; it is a fast, an aggravated fast, a scourge to indulgence, a reproach to gluttony; it comes Saturday night, and is followed Sunday morning by the dry, spongy, antiseptic, absorbent fish-ball as a castigation of nature and as a preparation for the austere observance of the Sabbath; it is the harsh, but no doubt deserved, punishment of the stomach for its worldliness during the week; inured to suffering, the native accepts the dose as a matter of course; to the stranger it seems unduly severe. To be sent to bed supperless is one of the terrors of childhood; to be sent to bed on pork and beans with the certainty of fishballs in the morning is a refinement of torture that could have been devised only by Puritan ingenuity.

At the very crisis of the trouble in China, when the whole world was anxiously awaiting news from Pekin, the papers said that Boston was perturbed by the reported discovery in Africa of a new and edible bean.

To New England the bean is an obsession; it is rapidly becoming a superstition. To the stranger it is an infliction; but, bad as the bean is to the uninitiated, it is a luscious morsel compared with the flavorless cod-fish ball which lodges in the throat and stays there — a second Adam's apple — for lack of something to wash it down.

If pork and beans is the device of the Puritans, the cod-fish ball is the invention of the devil. It is as if Satan looked on enviously while his foes prepared their powder of beans, and then, retiring to his bottomless pit, went them one better by casting his ball of cod-fish.

> "But from the parlor of the inn
> A pleasant murmur smote the ear,
> Like water rushing through a weir;
> Oft interrupted by the din
> Of laughter and of loud applause.
>
> "The firelight, shedding over all
> The splendor of its ruddy glow,
> Filled the whole parlor large and low."

The room remains, but of all that jolly company which gathered in Longfellow's days and constituted the imaginary weavers of tales and romances, but one is alive to-day, — the "Young Sicilian."

> "A young Sicilian, too, was there;
> In sight of Etna born and bred,
> Some breath of its volcanic air
> Was glowing in his heart and brain,
> And, being rebellious to his liege,
> After Palermo's fatal siege,
> Across the western seas he fled,
> In good king Bomba's happy reign.
> His face was like a summer night,
> All flooded with a dusky light;
> His hands were small; his teeth shone white
> As sea-shells, when he smiled or spoke."

To the present proprietor of the inn the "Young Sicilian" wrote the following letter:

Rome, July 4, 1898.

Dear Sir, — In answer to your letter of June 8, I am delighted to learn that you have purchased the dear old house and carefully restored and put it back in its old-time condition. I sincerely hope that it may remain thus for a long, long time as a memento of the days and customs gone by. It is very sad for me to think that I am the only living member of that happy company that used to spend their summer vacations there in the fifties; yet I still hope that I may visit the old Inn once more before I rejoin those choice spirits whom Mr. Longfellow has immortalized in his great poem. I am glad that some of the old residents still remember me when I was a visitor there with Dr. Parsons (the Poet), and his sisters, one of whom, my wife, is also the only living member of those who used to assemble there. Both my wife and I remember well Mr. Calvin Howe, Mr. Parmenter, and the others you mention: for we spent many summers there with Professor Treadwell (the Theologian) and his wife, Mr. Henry W. Wales (the Student), and other visitors not mentioned in the poem, till the death of Mr. Lyman Howe (the Landlord), which broke up the party. The "Musician" and the "Spanish Jew," though not imaginary characters, were never guests at the "Wayside Inn." I remain,

Sincerely yours,

Luigi Monti (the "Young Sicilian").

But there was a "Musician," for Ole Bull was once a guest at the Wayside,

"Fair-haired, blue-eyed, his aspect blithe,
His figure tall and straight and lithe,
And every feature of his face
Revealing his Norwegian race."

The "Spanish Jew from Alicant" in real life was Israel Edrehi.

The Landlord told his tale of Paul Revere; the "Student" followed with his story of love:

"Only a tale of love is mine,
Blending the human and divine,
A tale of the Decameron, told
In Palmieri's garden old."

And one by one the tales were told until the last was said.

"The hour was late; the fire burned low,
The Landlord's eyes were closed in sleep,
And near the story's end a deep
Sonorous sound at times was heard,
As when the distant bagpipes blow,
At this all laughed; the Landlord stirred,
As one awaking from a sound,
And, gazing anxiously around,
Protested that he had not slept,
But only shut his eyes, and kept
His ears attentive to each word.

Then all arose, and said 'Good-Night.'
Alone remained the drowsy Squire
To rake the embers of the fire,
And quench the waning parlor light;
While from the windows, here and there,
The scattered lamps a moment gleamed,
And the illumined hostel seemed
The constellation of the Bear,
Downward, athwart the misty air,
Sinking and setting toward the sun.
Far off the village clock struck one."

Before leaving the next morning, we visited the ancient ballroom which extends over the dining-room. It seemed crude and cruel to enter this hall of bygone revelry by the garish light of day. The two fireplaces were cold and inhospitable; the pen at one end where the fiddlers sat was deserted; the wooden benches which fringed the sides were hard and forbidding; but long before any of us were born this room was the scene of many revelries; the vacant hearths were bright with flame; the fiddlers bowed and scraped; the seats were filled with belles and beaux, and the stately minuet was danced upon the polished floor.

The large dining-room and ballroom were added to the house something more than a hundred years ago; the little old dining-room and old kitchen in the rear of the bar still remain, but — like the bar — are no longer used.

The brass name plates on the bedroom doors — Washington, Lafayette, Howe, and so on — have no significance, but were put on by the present proprietor simply as reminders that those great men were once beneath the roof; but in what rooms they slept or were entertained, history does not record.

The automobile will bring new life to these deserted hostelries. For more than half a century steam has diverted their custom, carrying former patrons from town to town without the need of half-way stops and rests. Coaching is a fad, not a fashion; it is not to be relied upon for steady custom; but automobiling bids fair to carry the people once more into the country, and there must be inns to receive them.

Already the proprietor was struggling with the problem what to do with automobiles and what to do for them who drove them. He was vainly endeavoring to reconcile the machines with horses and house them under one roof; the experiment had already borne fruit in some disaster and no little discomfort.

The automobile is quite willing to be left out-doors over night; but if taken inside it is quite apt to assert itself rather noisily and monopolize things to the discomfort of the horse. Stables — to rob the horse of the name of his home — must be provided, and these should be equipped for emergencies.

Every country inn should have on hand gasoline — this is easily stored outside in a tank buried in the ground — and lubricating oils for steam and gasoline machines; these can be kept and sold in gallon cans.

In addition to supplies there should be some tools, beginning with a good jack strong enough to lift the heaviest machine, a small bench and vise, files, chisels, punches, and one or two large wrenches, including a pipe-wrench. All these things can be purchased for little more than a song, and when needed they are needed badly. But gasoline and lubricating oils are absolutely essential to the permanent prosperity of any well-conducted wayside inn.

CHAPTER 15

Rhode Island and Connecticut

CALLING THE FERRY

Next morning, Sunday the 8th, we left the inn at eleven o'clock for Providence. It was a perfect morning, neither hot nor cold, sun bright, and the air stirring.

We took the narrow road almost opposite the entrance to the inn, climbed the hill, threaded the woods, and were soon travelling almost due south through Framingham, Holliston, Medway, Franklin, and West Wrentham towards Pawtucket.

That route is direct, the roads are good, the country rolling and interesting. The villages come in close succession; there are many quaint places and beautiful homes.

In this section of Massachusetts it does not matter much what roads are selected, they are all good. Some are macadamized, more are gravelled, and where there is neither macadam nor gravel, the roads have been so carefully thrown up that they are good; we found no bad places at all, no deep sand, and no rough, hard blue clay.

When we stopped for luncheon at a little village not far from Pawtucket, the tire which had been put on in Boston was leaking badly. It was the tire that had been punctured and sent to the factory for repairs, and the repair proved defective. We managed to get to Pawtucket, and there tried to stop the leak with liquid preparations, but by the time we reached Providence the tire was again flat and — as it proved afterwards — ruined.

Had it not been for the tire, Narragansett Pier would have been made that afternoon with ease; but there was nothing to do but wire for a new tire and await its arrival.

It was not until half-past three o'clock Monday that the new one came from New York, and it was five when we left for the Pier.

The road from Providence to Narragansett Pier is something more than fair, considerably less than fine; it is hilly and in places quite sandy. For some distance out of Providence it was dusty and worn rough by heavy travel.

It was seven o'clock, dark and quite cold, when we drew up in front of Green's Inn.

The season was over, the Pier quite deserted. A summer resort after the guests have gone is a mournful, or a delightful, place — as one views it. To the gregarious individual who seeks and misses his kind, the place is loneliness itself after the flight of the gay birds who for a time strutted about in gorgeous plumage twittering the time away; to the man who loves to be in close and undisturbed contact with nature, who enjoys communing with the sea, who would be alone on the beach and silent by the waves, the flight of the throng is a relief. There is a selfish satisfaction in passing the great summer caravansaries and seeing them closed and silent; in knowing that the splendor of the night will not be marred by garish lights and still more garish sounds.

Were it not for the crowd, Narragansett Pier would be an ideal spot for rest and recreation. The beach is perfect, — hard, firm sand, sloping so gradually into deep water, and with so little undertow and so few dangers, that children can play in the water without attendants. The village itself is inoffensive, the country about is attractive; but the crowd — the crowd that comes in summer — comes with a rush almost to the hour in July, and takes flight with a greater rush almost to the minute in August, — the crowd overwhelms, submerges, ignores the natural charms of the place, and for the time being nature hides its honest head before the onrush of sham and illusion.

Why do the people come in a week and go in a day? What is there about Narragansett that keeps everyone away until a certain time each year, attracts them for a few weeks, and then bids them off within twenty-four hours? Just nothing at all. All attractions the place has — the ocean, the beach, the drives, the country — remain the same; but no one dares come before the appointed time, no one dares stay after the flight begins; no one? That is hardly true, for in every beautiful spot, by the ocean and in the mountains, there are a few appreciative souls who know enough to make their homes in nature's caressing embrace while she works for their pure enjoyment her wondrous panorama of changing seasons. There are people who linger at the sea-shore until from the steel-gray waters are heard the first mutterings of approaching winter; there are those who linger in the woods and mountains until the green of summer yields to the rich browns and golden russets of autumn, until the honk of the wild goose foretells the coming cold; these and their kind are nature's truest and dearest friends; to them does she unfold a thousand hidden beauties; to them does she whisper her most precious secrets.

But the crowd — the crowd — the painted throng that steps to the tune of a fiddle, that hangs on the moods of a caterer, whose inspiration is a good dinner, whose aspiration is a new dance, — that crowd is never missed by anyone who really delights in the manifold attractions of nature.

Not that the crowd at Narragansett is essentially other than the crowd at Newport — the two do not mix; but the difference is one of degree rather than kind. The crowd at Newport is architecturally perfect, while the crowd at Narragansett is in the adobe stage, — that is the conspicuous difference; the one is pretentious and lives in structures more or less permanent; the other lives in trunks, and is even more pretentious. Neither, as a crowd, has more than a superficial regard for the natural charms of its surroundings. The people at both places are entirely preoccupied with themselves — and their neighbors. At Newport a reputation is like an umbrella — lost, borrowed, lent, stolen, but never returned. Someone has cleverly said that the American girl, unlike girls of European extraction, if she loses her reputation, promptly goes and gets another, — to be strictly accurate, she promptly goes and gets another's. What a world of bother could be saved if a woman could check her reputation with her wraps on entering the Casino; for, no matter how small the reputation, it is so annoying to have the care of it during social festivities where it is not wanted, or where, like dogs, it is forbidden the premises. Then, too, if the reputation happens to be somewhat soiled, stained, or tattered, — like an old opera cloak, — what woman wants it about. It is difficult to sit on it, as on a wrap in a theatre; it is conspicuous to hold in the lap where everyone may see its imperfections; perhaps the safest thing is to do as many a woman does, ask her escort to look out for it, thereby shifting the responsibility to him. It may pass through strange vicissitudes in his careless hands, — he may drop it, damage it, lose it, even destroy it, but she is reasonably sure that when the time comes he will return her either the old in a tolerable state of preservation, or a new one of some kind in its place.

Narragansett possesses this decided advantage over Newport, the people do not know each other until it is too late. For six weeks the gay little world moves on in blissful ignorance of antecedents and reputations; no questions are asked, no information volunteered save that disclosed by the hotel register, — information frequently of apocryphal value. The gay beau of the night may be the industrious clerk of the morrow; the baron of the summer may be the barber of the winter; but what difference does it make? If the beau beaus and the baron barons, is not the feminine cup of happiness filled to overflowing? the only requisite being that beau and baron shall preserve their incognito to the end; hence the season must be short in order that no one's identity may be discovered.

At Newport everyone labors under the disadvantage of being known, — for the most part too well known. How painful it must be to spend summer after summer in a world of reality, where the truth is so much more thrilling than any possible fiction that people are deprived of the pleasure of invention and the imagination falls into desuetude. At Narragansett everyone is veneered for the occasion, — every seam, scar, and furrow is hidden by paint, powder, and rouge; the duchess may be a cook, but the count who is a butler gains nothing by exposing her.

The very conditions of existence at Newport demand the exposure of every frailty and every folly; the skeleton must sit at the feast. There is no room for gossip where the facts are known. Nothing is whispered; the megaphone carries the tale. What a ghastly society, where no amount of finery hides the bald, the literal truth; where each night the same ones meet and, despite the vain attempt to deceive by outward appearances, relentlessly look each other through and through. Of what avail is a necklace of pearls or a gown of gold against such X-ray vision, such intimate knowledge of one's past, of all one's physical, mental, and moral shortcomings? The smile fades from the lips, the hollow compliment dies on the tongue, for how is it possible to pretend in the presence of those who know?

At Narragansett friends are strangers, in Newport they are enemies; in both places the quality of friendship is strained. The two problems of existence are, Whom shall I recognize? and, Who will recognize me? A man's standing depends upon the women he knows; a woman's upon the women she cuts. At a summer resort recognition is a fine art which is not affected by any prior condition of servitude or acquaintance. No woman can afford to sacrifice her position upon the altar of friendship; in these small worlds recognition has no relation whatsoever to friendship, it is rather a convention. If your hostess of the winter passes you with a cold stare, it is a matter of prudence rather than indifference; the outside world does not understand these things, but is soon made to.

Women are the arbiters of social fate, and as such must be placated, but not too servilely. In society a blow goes farther than a kiss; it is a warfare wherein it does not pay to be on the defensive; those are revered who are most feared; those who nail to their mast the black flag and show no quarter are the recognized leaders, — Society is piracy.

Green's Inn was cheery, comfortable, and hospitable; but then the season had passed and things had returned to their normal routine.

The summer hotel passes through three stages each season, — that of expectation, of realization, and of regret; it is unpleasant during the first stage, intolerable during the second, frequently delightful during the third. During the first there is a period when the host and guest meet on a footing of equality; during the second the guest is something less than a nonentity, an humble suitor at the monarch's throne; during the third the conditions are reversed, and the guest is lord of all he is willing to survey. It is conducive to comfort to approach these resorts during the last stage, — unless, of course, they happen to be those caravansaries which close in confusion on the flight of the crowd; they are never comfortable.

The best road from Boston to New York is said to be by way of Worcester, Springfield, and through central Connecticut via Hartford and New Haven; but we did not care to retrace our wheels to Worcester and Springfield, and we did want to follow the shore; but we were warned by many that after leaving the Pier we would find the roads very bad.

As a matter of fact, the shore road from the Pier to New Haven is not good; it is hilly, sandy, and rough; but it is entirely practicable, and makes up in beauty and interest what it lacks in quality.

We did not leave Green's Inn until half-past nine the morning after our arrival, and we reached New Haven that evening at exactly eight, — a delightful run of eighty or ninety miles by the road taken.

The road is a little back from the shore and it is anything but straight, winding in and out in the effort to keep near the coast. Nearly all day long we were in sight of the ocean; now and then some wooded promontory obscured our view; now and then we were threading woods and valleys farther inland; now and then the road almost lost itself in thickets of shrubbery and undergrowth, but each time we would emerge in sight of the broad expanse of blue water which lay like a vast mirror on that bright and still September day.

We ferried across the river to New London. At Lyme there is a very steep descent to the Connecticut River, which is a broad estuary at that point. The ferry is a primitive side-wheeler, which might carry two automobiles, but hardly more. It happened to be on the far shore. A small boy pointed out a long tin horn hanging on a post, the hoarse blast of which summons the sleepy boat.

There was no landing, and it seemed impossible for our vehicle to get aboard; but the boat had a long shovel-like nose projecting from the bow which ran upon the shore, making a perfect gang-plank.

Carefully balancing the automobile in the centre so as not to list the primitive craft, we made our way deliberately to the other side, the entire crew of two men — engineer and captain — coming out to talk with us.

The ferries at Lyme and New London would prove great obstacles to anything like a club from New York to Newport along this road; the day would be spent in getting machines across the two rivers.

It was dark when we ran into the city. This particular visit to New Haven is chiefly memorable for the exceeding good manners of a boy of ten, who watched the machine next morning as it was prepared for the day's ride, offered to act as guide to the place where gasoline was kept, and, with the grace of a Chesterfield, made good my delinquent purse by paying the bill. It was all charmingly and not precociously done. This little man was well brought up, — so well brought up that he did not know it.

The automobile is a pretty fair touchstone to manners for both young and old. A man is himself in the presence of the unexpected. The automobile is so strange that it carries people off their equilibrium, and they say and do things impulsively, and therefore naturally.

The odd-looking stranger is ever treated with scant courtesy and unbecoming curiosity; the strange machine fares no better. The man or the boy who is not unduly curious, not unduly aggressive, not unduly loquacious, not unduly insistent, who preserves his poise in the presence of an automobile, is quite out of the ordinary, — my little New Haven friend was of that sort.

It is a beautiful ride from New Haven to New York, and to it we devoted the entire day, from half-past eight until half-past seven.

At Norwalk the people were celebrating the two hundred and fiftieth anniversary of the founding of the town; the hotel where we dined may have antedated the town a century or two.

Later in the afternoon, while wheeling along at twenty miles an hour, we caught a glimpse of a signpost pointing to the left and reading, "To Sound Beach." The name reminded us of friends who were spending a few weeks there; we turned back and made them a flying call.

Again a little farther on we stopped for gasoline in a dilapidated little village, and found it was Mianus, which we recalled as the home of an artist whose paintings, full of charm and tender sentiment, have spread the fame of the locality and river. It was only a short run of two or three miles to the orchard and hill where he has his summer home, and we renewed an acquaintance made several years before.

It is interesting to follow an artist's career and note the changes in manner and methods; for changes are inevitable; they come to high and low alike. The artist may not be conscious that he no longer sees things and paints things as he did, but time tells and the truth is patent to others. But changes of manner and changes of method are fundamentally unlike. Furthermore, changes of either manner or method may be unconscious and natural, or conscious and forced.

For the most part, an artist's manner changes naturally and unconsciously with his environment and advancing years; but in the majority of instances changes in method are conscious and forced, made deliberately with the intention — frequently missed — of doing better. One painter is impressed with the success of another and strives to imitate, adopts his methods, his palette, his key, his color scheme, his brush work, and so on; — these conscious efforts of imitation usually result in failures which, if not immediately conspicuous, soon make their shortcomings felt; the note being forced and unnatural, it does not ring true.

A man may visit Madrid without imitating Velasquez; he may live in Harlem without consciously yielding to Franz Hals; he may spend days with Monet without surrendering his independence; but these strong contacts will work their subtle effects upon all impressionable natures; the effects, however, may be wrought unconsciously and frequently against the sturdy opposition of an original nature.

No painter could live for a season in Madrid without being affected by the work of Velasquez; he might strive against the influence, fight to preserve his own eccentric originality and independence, but the very fact that for the time being he is confronted with a force, an influence, is sufficient to affect his own work, whether he accepts the influence reverentially or rejects it scoffingly.

There is infinitely more hope for the man who goes to Madrid, or any other shrine, in a spirit of opposition, — supremely egotistical, supremely confident of his own methods, disposed to belittle the teaching and example of others, — than there is for the man who goes to servilely copy and imitate. The disposition to learn is a good thing, but in all walks of life, as well as in art, it may be carried too far. No man should surrender his individuality, should yield that within him which is peculiarly and essentially his own. An urchin may dispute with a Plato, if the urchin sticks to the things he knows.

Between the lawless who defy all authority and the servile who submit to all influences, there are the chosen few who assert themselves, and at the same time clearly appreciate the strength of those who differ from them. The urchin painter may assert himself in the presence of Velasquez, providing he keeps within the limits of his own originality.

It is for those who buy pictures to look out for the man who arbitrarily and suddenly changes his manner or method; he is as a cork tossed about on the surface of the waters, drifting with every breeze, submerged by every ripple, fickle and unstable; if his work possess any merit, it will be only the cheap merit of cleverness; its brilliancy will be simply the gloss of dash.

It requires time to absorb an impression. Distance diminishes the force of attraction. The best of painters will not regain immediately his equilibrium after a winter in Florence or in Rome. The enthusiasm of the hour may bring forth some good pictures, but the effect of the impression will be too pronounced, the copy will be too evident. Time and distance will modify an impression and lessen the attraction; the effect will remain, but no longer dominate.

It was so dark we could scarcely see the road as we approached New York.

How gracious the mantle of night; like a veil it hides all blemishes and permits only fair outlines to be observed. Details are lost in vast shadows; huge buildings loom up vaguely towards the heavens, impressive masses of masonry; the bridges, outlined by rows of electric lights, are strings of pearls about the throat of the dusky river. The red, white, and green lights of invisible boats below are so many colored glow-worms crawling about, while the countless lights of the vast city itself are as if a constellation from above had settled for the time being on the earth beneath.

It is by night that the earth communes with the universe. During the blinding brightness of the day our vision penetrates no farther than our own great sun; but at night, when our sun has run its course across the heavens, and we are no longer dazzled by its overpowering brilliancy, the suns of other worlds come forth one by one until, as the darkness deepens, the vault above is dotted with these twinkling lights. Dim, distant, beacons of suns and planets like our own, what manner of life do they contain? what are we to them? what are they to us? Is there aught between us beyond the mechanical laws of repulsion and attraction? Is there any medium of communication beyond the impalpable ether which brings their light? Are we destined to know each other better by and by, or does our knowledge forever end with what we see on a cloudless night?

It was Wednesday evening, September 11, when we arrived in New York. The Endurance Contest organized by the Automobile Club of America had started for Buffalo on Monday morning, and the papers each day contained long accounts of the heartbreaking times the eighty-odd contestants were having, — hills, sand, mud, worked havoc in the ranks of the faithful, and by midweek the automobile stations in New York were crowded with sick and wounded veterans returning from the fray.

The stories told by those who participated in that now famous run possessed the charm of novelty, the absorbing fascination of fiction.

Once upon a time, two fishermen, who were modestly relating exploits, paused to listen to three chauffeurs who began exchanging experiences. After listening a short time, the fishermen, hats in hand, went over to the chauffeurs and said, "On behalf of the Ancient and Honorable Order of Fishermen, which from time immemorial has held the palm for large, generous, and unrestricted stories of exploits, we confess the inadequacy of our qualifications, the bald literalness of our narratives, the sober and unadorned realism of our tales, and abdicate in favor of the new and most promising Order of Chauffeurs; may the blessing of Ananias rest upon you."

It is not that those who go down the pike in automobiles intend to prevaricate, or even exaggerate, but the experience is so extraordinary that the truth is inadequate for expression and explanation. It seems quite impossible to so adjust our perceptions as to receive strictly accurate impressions; therefore, when one man says he went forty miles an hour, and another says he went sixty, the latter assertion is based not upon the exact speed, — for that neither knows, — but upon the belief of the second man that he went much faster than the other. The exact speeds were probably about ten and fifteen miles an hour respectively; but the ratio is preserved in forty and sixty, and the listening layman is deeply impressed, while no one who knows anything about automobiling is for a moment deceived. At the same time, in fairness to guests and strangers within the gates, each club ought to post conspicuously the rate of discount on narratives, for not only do clubs vary in their departures from literal truth, but the narratives are greatly affected by seasons and events; for instance, after the Endurance Contest the discount rate in the Automobile Club of America was exceedingly high.

Every man who started finished ahead of the others, — except those who never intended to finish at all. Each man went exactly as far as he intended to go, and then took the train, road, or ditch home. Some intended to go as far as Albany, others to Frankfort, while quite a large number entered the contest for the express purpose of getting off in the mud and walking to the nearest village; a few, a very few, intended to go as far as Buffalo.

At one time or another each made a mile a minute, and a much higher rate of speed would have been maintained throughout had it not been necessary to identify certain towns in passing. Nothing happened to any machine, but one or two required a little oiling, and several were abandoned by the roadside because their occupants had stubbornly determined to go no farther. One man who confessed that a set-screw in his goggles worked loose was expelled from the club as too matter-of-fact to be eligible for membership, and the maker of the machine he used sent four-page communications to each trade paper explaining that the loosening of the set-screw was due to no defect in the machine, but was entirely the fault of the driver, who jarred the screw loose by winking his eye.

Each machine surmounted Nelson Hill like a bird, — or would have, if it had not been for the machine in front There were those who would have made the hill in forty-two seconds if they had not wasted valuable time in pushing. The pitiful feat of the man who crawled up at the rate of seventeen miles an hour was quite discounted by the stories of those who would have made it in half that time if their power had not oozed out in the first hundred yards.

Then there was mud along the route, deep mud. According to accounts, which were eloquently verified by the silence of all who listened, the mud was hub deep everywhere, and in places the machines were quite out of sight, burrowing like moles. Some took to the tow-path along the canal, others to trolley lines and telegraph wires.

Each man ran his own machine without the slightest expert assistance; the men in over-alls with kits of tools lurking along the roadside were modern brigands seeking opportunities for hold-ups; now and then they would spring out upon an unoffending machine, knock it into a state of insensibility, and abuse it most unmercifully. A number of machines were shadowed throughout the run by these rascals, and several did not escape their clutches, but perished miserably. In one instance a babe in arms drove one machine sixty-two miles an hour with one hand, the other being occupied with a nursing-bottle.

There were one hundred and fifty-six dress-suit cases on the run, but only one was used, and that to sit on during high tide in Herkimer County, where the mud was deepest.

It would be quite superfluous to relate additional experience tales, but enough has been told to illustrate the necessity of a narrative discount notice in all places where the clans gather. All men are liars, but some intend to lie, — to their credit, be it said, chauffeurs are not among the latter.

CHAPTER 16

Anarchism

"BULLETINS FROM THE CHAMBER OF DEATH"
During these days the President was dying in Buffalo, though the country did not know it until Friday.

Wednesday and Thursday the reports were so assuring that all danger seemed past; but, as it turned out afterwards, there was not a moment from the hour of the shooting when the fatal processes of dissolution were not going on. Not only did the resources of surgery and medicine fail most miserably, but their gifted prophets were unable to foretell the end. Bulletins of the most reassuring character turned out absolutely false. After it was all over, there was a great deal of explanation how it occurred and that it was inevitable from the beginning; but the public did not, and does not, understand how the learned doctors could have been so mistaken Wednesday and so wise Friday; and yet the explanation is simple, — medicine is an art and surgery far from an exact science. No one so well as the doctors knows how impossible it is to predict anything with any degree of assurance; how uncertain the outcome of simple troubles and wounds to say nothing of serious; how much nature will do if left to herself, how obstinate she often proves when all the skill of man is brought to her assistance.

On Friday evening, and far into the night, Herald Square was filled with a surging throng watching the bulletins from the chamber of death. It was a dignified end. There must have been a good deal of innate nobility in William McKinley. With all his vacillation and infirmity of political purpose, he must have been a man whose mind was saturated with fine thoughts, for to the very last, in those hours of weakness when the will no longer sways and each word is the half-unconscious muttering of the true self, he shone forth with unexpected grandeur and died a hero.

Late in the evening a bulletin announced that when the message of death came the bells would toll. In the midst of the night the city was roused by the solemn pealing of great bells, and from the streets below there came the sounds of flying horses, of moving feet, of cries and voices. it seemed as if the city had been held in check and was now released to express itself in its own characteristic way. The wave of sound radiated from each newspaper office and penetrated the most deserted street, the most secret alley, telling the people of the death of their President.

Anarchy achieved its greatest crime in the murder of President McKinley while he held the hand of his assassin in friendly grasp.

Little wonder this country was roused as never before, and at this moment the civilized world is discussing measures for the suppression, the obliteration, of anarchists, but we must take heed lest we overshoot the mark.

Three Presidents—Lincoln, Garfield, and McKinley—have been assassinated, but only the last as the result of anarchistic teachings. The crime of Booth had nothing to do with anarchy; the crime of half-witted Guiteau had nothing to do with anarchy; but the deliberate crime of the cool and self-possessed Czolgoscz was the direct outcome of the "propaganda of action."

Because, therefore, three Presidents have been assassinated, we must not link the crimes together and unduly magnify the dangers of anarchy. At most the two early crimes could only serve to demonstrate how easy it is to reach and kill a President of the United States, and therefore the necessity for greater safeguards about his person is trebly demonstrated. The habit of handshaking, at best, has little to recommend it; with public men it is a custom without excuse. The notion that men in public life must receive and mingle with great masses of people, or run the risk of being called undemocratic, is a relic of the political dark ages. The President of the United States is an executive official, not a spectacle; he ought to be a very busy man, just a plain, hard-working servant of the people, —that is the real democratic idea. There is not the slightest need for him to expose himself to assault. In the proper performance of his duties he ought to keep somewhat aloof. The people have the right to expect that in their interest he will take good care of himself.

As for anarchism, that is a political theory that possesses the minds of a certain number of men, some of them entirely inoffensive dreamers, and anarchism as a theory can no more be suppressed by law than can any other political or religious theory. The law is efficacious against acts, but powerless against notions. But anarchism in the abstract is one thing and anarchism in the concrete is another. It is one thing to preach anarchy as the final outcome of progress, it is quite another thing to preach anarchy as a present rule of conduct. The distinction must be observed, for while the law is helpless against theories, it is potent against the practical application of theories.

In a little book called "Politics for Young Americans," written with most pious and orthodox intent by the late Charles Nordhoff, the discussion of government begins with the epigram, — by no means original with Nordhoff, — "Governments are necessary evils."

Therein lurks the germ of anarchism, — for if evil, why should governments be necessary? The anarchist is quick to admit the evil, but denies the necessity; and, in sooth, if government is an evil, then the sooner it is dispensed with the better.

When Huxley defines anarchy as that "state of society in which the rule of each individual by himself is the only government the legitimacy of which is recognized," and then goes onto say, "in this sense, strict anarchy may be the highest conceivable grade of perfection of social existence; for, if all men spontaneously did justice and loved mercy, it is plain that the swords might advantageously be turned into ploughshares, and that the occupation of judges and police would be gone," he lends support to the theoretical anarchist. For if progress means the gradual elimination of government and the final supremacy of the individual, then the anarchist is simply the prophet who keeps in view and preaches the end. If anarchy is an ideal condition, there always will be idealists who will advocate it.

But government is necessary, and just because it is necessary therefore it cannot be an evil. Hospitals are necessary, and just because they are necessary therefore they cannot be evils. Places for restraining the insane and criminal are necessary, and therefore not evil.

The weaknesses of humanity may occasion these necessities; but the evil, if any, is inherent in the constitution of man and not in the social organization. It is the individual and not society that has need of government, of hospitals, of asylums, of prisons.

Anarchy does not involve, as Huxley suggests, "the highest conceivable grade of perfection of social existence." Not at all. What it does involve is the highest conceivable grade of individual existence; in fact, of a grade so high that it is quite beyond conception, — in short, it involves human perfectibility. Anarchy proper involves the complete emancipation of every individual from all restraints and compulsions; it involves a social condition wherein absolutely no authority is imposed upon any individual,

where no requirement of any kind is made against the will of any member
— man, woman, or child; where everything is left to individual initiation.

So far from such a "state of society" being "the highest conceivable
grade of perfection of social existence," it is not conceivable at all, and the
farther the mind goes in attempting to grasp it, the more hopelessly dreary
does the scheme become.

When men spontaneously do justice and love mercy, as Huxley suggests, and when each individual is mentally, physically, and morally
sound, as he must be to support and govern himself, then, and not till
then, will it be possible to dispense with government; but even then it is
more conceivable than otherwise that these perfect individuals would —
as a mere division of labor, as a mere matter of economy — adopt and
enforce some rules and regulations for the benefit of all; it would be
necessary to do so unless the individuals were not only perfect, but also
absolutely of one mind on all subjects relating to their welfare. Can the
imagination picture existence more inane?

But regardless of what the mentally, physically, and morally perfect
individuals might do after attaining their perfection, anarchy assumes the
millennium, — and the millennium is yet a long way off. If the future of
anarchy depends upon the physical, mental, and moral perfection of its
advocates, the outlook is gloomy indeed, for a theory never had a following more imperfect in all these respects.

The patent fact that most governments, both national and local, are
corruptly, extravagantly, and badly administered tends to obscure our
judgment, so that we assent, without thinking, to the proposition that
government is an evil, and then argue that it is a necessary evil. But government is not evil because there are evils incidental to its administration.
Every human institution partakes of the frailties of the individual; it could
not be otherwise; all social institutions are human, not superhuman.

With progress it is to be hoped that there will be fewer wars, fewer
crimes, fewer wrongs, so that government will have less and less to do and
drop many of its functions, — that is the sort of anarchy everyone hopes
for; that is the sort of anarchy the late Phillips Brooks had in mind when
he said, "He is the benefactor of his race who makes it possible to have
one law less. He is the enemy of his kind who would lay upon the shoulders of arbitrary government one burden which might be carried by the
educated conscience and character of the community."

But assume that war is no more and armies are disbanded; that crimes are no more and police are dismissed; that wrongs are no more and courts are dissolved, — what then?

My neighbor becomes slightly insane, is very noisy and threatening; my wife and children, who are terrorized, wish him restrained; but his friends do not admit that he is insane, or, admitting his peculiarities, insist my family and I ought to put up with them; the man himself is quite sane enough to appreciate the discussion and object to any restraint. Now, who shall decide? Suppose the entire community — save the man and one or two sympathizing cranks — is clearly of the opinion the man is insane and should be restrained, who is to decide the matter? and when it is decided, who is to enforce the decision by imposing the authority of the community upon the individual? If the community asserts its authority in any manner or form, that is government.

If every institution, including government, were abolished tomorrow, the percentage of births that would turn out blind, crippled, and feeble both mentally and physically, wayward, eccentric, and insane would continue practically the same, and the community would be obliged to provide institutions for these unfortunates, the community would be obliged to patrol the streets for them, the community would be obliged to pass upon their condition and support or restrain them; in short, the abolished institutions — including tribunals of some kind, police, prisons, asylums — would be promptly restored.

The anarchist would argue that all this may be done by voluntary association and without compulsion; but the man arrested, or confined in the insane asylum against his will, would be of a contrary opinion. The debate might involve his friends and sympathizers until in every close case — as now — the community would be divided in hostile camps, one side urging release of the accused, the other urging his detention. Who is to hold the scale and decide?

The fundamental error of anarchists, and of most theorists who discuss "government" and "the state," lies in the tacit assumption that "government" and "the state" are entities to be dealt with quite apart from the individual; that both may be modified or abolished by laws or resolutions to that effect.

If anything is clearly demonstrated as true, it is that both "government" and "the state" have been evolved out of our own necessities; neither was imposed from without, but both have been evolved from within; both are forms of co-operation. For the time being the "state" and "government," as well as the "church" and all human institutions, may be modified or seemingly abolished, but they come back to serve essentially the same purpose. The French Revolution was an organized attempt to overturn the foundations of society and hasten progress by moving the hands of the clock forward a few centuries, — the net result was a despotism the like of which the world has not known since the days of Rome.

Anarchy as a system is a bubble, the iridescent hues of which attract, but which vanish into thin air on the slightest contact with reality; it is the perpetual motion of sociology; the fourth dimension of economies; the squaring of the political circle.

The apostles of anarchy are a queer lot, — Godwin in England, Proudhon, Grave, and Saurin in France, Schmidt ("Stirner"), Faucher, Hess, and Marr in Germany, Bakunin and Krapotkin in Russia, Reclus in Belgium, with Most and Tucker in America, sum up the principal lights, —with the exception of the geographer Reclus, not a sound and sane man among them; in fact, scarcely any two agree upon a single proposition save the broad generalization that government is an evil which must be eliminated. Until they do agree upon some one measure or proposition of practical importance, the world has little to fear from their discussions and there is no reason why any attempt should be made to suppress the debate. If government is an evil, as so many men who are not anarchists keep repeating, then the sooner we know it and find the remedy the better; but if government is simply one of many human institutions developed logically and inevitably to meet conditions created by individual shortcomings, then government will tend to diminish as we correct our own failings, but that it will entirely disappear is hardly likely, since it is inconceivable that men on this earth should ever attain such a condition of perfection that possibility of disagreement is absolutely and forever removed.

Anarchism as a doctrine, as a theory, involves no act of violence any more than communism or socialism.

Between the assassination of a ruler and the doctrine of anarchy there is no necessary connection. The philosophic anarchist simply believes anarchy is to be the final result of progress and evolution, just as the communist believes that communism will be the outcome; neither theorist would see the slightest advantage in trying to hasten the slow but sure progress of events by deeds of violence; in fact, both theorists would regret such deeds as certain to prove reactionary and retard the march of events.

The world has nothing to fear from anarchism as a theory, and up to thirty or forty years ago it was nothing but a theory.

The "propaganda of action" came out of Russia about forty years ago, and is the offspring of Russian nihilism.

The "propaganda of action" is the protest of impatience against evolution; it is the effort to hasten progress by deeds of violence.

From the few who, like Bakunin, Brousse, and Krapotkin, have written about the "propaganda of action" with sufficient coherence to make themselves understood, it appears that it is not their hope to destroy government by removing all executive heads, — even their tortured brains recognize the impossibility of that task; nor do they hope to so far terrify rulers as to bring about their abdication. Not at all; but they do hope by deeds of violence to so attract attention to the theory of anarchy as to win followers; — in other words, murders such as those of Humbert, Carnot, and President McKinley were mere advertisements of anarchism. In the words of Brousse, "Deeds are talked of on all sides; the indifferent masses inquire about their origin, and thus pay attention to the new doctrine and discuss it. Let men once get as far as this, and it is not hard to win over many of them."

Hence, the greater the crime the greater the advertisement; from that point of view, the shooting of President McKinley, under circumstances so atrocious, is so far the greatest achievement of the "propaganda of action."

It is worth noting that the "reign of terror" which the Nihilists sought to and did create in Russia was for a far more practical and immediate purpose. They sought to terrify the government into granting reforms; so far from seeking to annihilate the government, they sought to spur it into activity for the benefit of the masses.

The methods of the Nihilists, without the excuse of their object, were borrowed by the more fanatical anarchists, and applied to the advertising of their belief. Since the adoption of the "propaganda of action" by the extremists, anarchism has undergone a great change. It has passed from a visionary and harmless theory, as advocated by Godwin, Proudhon, and Reclus, to a very concrete agency of crime and destruction under the teachings of such as Bakunin, Krapotkin, and Most; not forgetting certain women like Louise Michel in France and Emma Goldman in this country who out-Herod Herod; — when a woman goes to the devil she frightens him; his Satanic majesty welcomes a man, but dreads a woman; to a woman the downward path is a toboggan slide, to a man it is a gentle but seductive descent.

It is against the "propaganda of action" that legislation must be directed, not because it is any part of anarchism, but because it is the propaganda of crime.

Laws directed towards the suppression of anarchism might result in more harm than good, but crime is quite another matter. It is one thing to advocate less and less of government, to preach the final disappearance of government and the evolution of anarchy; it is a fundamentally different thing to advocate the destruction of life or property as a means to hasten the end.

The criminal action and the criminal advice must be dissociated entirely from any political or social theory. It does not matter what a man's ultimate purpose may be; he may be a communist or a socialist, a Republican or a Democrat, a Presbyterian or an Episcopalian; when he advises, commits, or condones a murder, his conduct is not measured by his convictions,—unless, of course, he is insane; his advice is measured by its probable and actual consequences; his deeds speak for themselves.

A man is not to be punished or silenced for saying he believes in anarchy, his convictions on that point are a matter of indifference to those who believe otherwise. But a man is to be punished for saying or doing things which result in injuring others; and the advice, whether given in person to the individual who commits the deed, or given generally in lecture or print, if it moves the individual to action, is equally criminal.

On August 20, 1886, eight men were found guilty of murder in Chicago, seven were condemned to death and one to the penitentiary; four were afterwards hanged, one killed himself in jail, and three were imprisoned.

These men were convicted of a crime with which, so far as the evidence showed, they had no direct connection; but their speeches, writings, and conduct prior to the actual commission of the crime had been such that they were held guilty of having incited the murder.

During the spring of 1886 there were many strikes and a great deal of excitement growing out of the "eight-hour movement in Chicago." There was much disorder. On the evening of May 4 a meeting was held in what was known as Haymarket Square, at this meeting three of the condemned made speeches. About ten o'clock a platoon of police marched to the Square, halted a short distance from the wagon where the speakers were, and an officer commanded the meeting to immediately and peaceably disperse. Thereupon a bomb was thrown from near the wagon into the ranks of the policemen, where it exploded, killing and wounding a number.

The man who threw the bomb was never positively identified, but it was probably one Rudolph Schnaubelt, who disappeared. At all events, the condemned were not connected with the actual throwing; they were convicted upon the theory that they were co-conspirators with him by reason of their speeches, writings, and conduct which influenced his conduct.

An even broader doctrine of liability is announced in the following paragraph from the opinion of the Supreme Court of Illinois:

"If the defendants, as a means of bringing about the social revolution and as a part of the larger conspiracy to effect such revolution, also conspired to excite classes of workingmen in Chicago into sedition, tumult, and riot, and to the use of deadly weapons and the taking of human life, and for the purpose of producing such tumult, riot, use of weapons and taking of life, advised and encouraged such classes by newspaper articles and speeches to murder the authorities of the city, and a murder of a policeman resulted from such advice and encouragement, then defendants are responsible therefor."

It is the logical application of this proposition that will defeat the "propaganda of action." If it be enacted that any man who advocates the commission of any criminal act, or who afterwards condones the crime, shall be deemed guilty of an offence equal to that advocated or condoned and punished accordingly, the "propaganda of action" in all branches of criminal endeavor will be effectually stifled without the doubtful expedient of directing legislation against any particular social or economic theory.

CHAPTER 17

New York to Buffalo

UP THE HILL

It was Saturday, the 14th, at nine o'clock, when we left New York for Albany, following the route of the Endurance Contest.

The morning was bright and warm. The roads were perfect for miles. We passed Kings Bridge, Yonkers, Hastings, and Dobbs Ferry flying. At Tarrytown we dropped the chain. A link had parted. Pushing the machine under the shade of a tree, a half-hour was spent in replacing the chain and riveting in a new link. All the pins showed more or less wear, and a new chain should have been put on in New York, but none that would fit was to be had.

We dined at Peekskill, and had a machinist go over the chain, riveting the heads of the pins so none would come out again.

Nelson Hill, a mile and a half beyond Peekskill, proved all it was said to be, — and more.

In the course of the trip we had mounted hills that were worse, and hills that were steeper, but only in spots or for short distances; for a steady steep climb Nelson Hill surpassed anything we found in the entire trip. The hill seems one-half to three-quarters of a mile long, a sharp ascent, — somewhat steeper about half-way up than at the beginning or finish. Accurate measurements were made for the Endurance Contest and the results published.

The grade was just a little too much for the machine, with our luggage and ourselves. It was tiresome walking so far beside the machine, and in attempting to bring it to a stop for a moment's rest the machine got started backward, and was well on its way down the hill, gaining speed every fraction of a second. It was a short, sharp chase to catch the lever operating the emergency brake, — which luckily operated by being pushed forward from the seat, — a pull on the lever and the machine was brought to a stop with the rear wheels hanging over the edge of a gulley at the side.

After that experience the machine was allowed to go to the top without any more attempts to rest.

At Fishkill Village we saved a few miles and some bad road by continuing on to Poughkeepsie by the inland road instead of going down to the Landing.

We inquired the way from an old man, who said, "If you want to go to P'keepsie, follow the road just this side the post-office; you will save a good many miles, and have a good road; if you want to follow the other fellers, then keep straight on down to the Landing; but why they went down there, beats me."

It was six-thirty when we arrived at Poughkeepsie. As the next day would be Sunday, we made sure of a supply of gasoline that night.

Up to this point the roads, barring Nelson Hill, and the weather had been perfect, but conditions were about to change for the worse.

Sunday morning was gray and drizzly. We left at eight-thirty. The roads were soft and in places very slippery; becoming much worse as we approached Albany, where we arrived at half-past three. There we should have stopped. We had come seventy-five miles in seven hours, including all stops, over bad roads, and that should have sufficed; but it was such an effort to house the machine in Albany and get settled in rooms, that we decided to go on at least as far as Schenectady.

To the park it was all plain sailing on asphalt and macadam, but from the park to the gate of the cemetery and to the turn beyond the mud was so deep and sticky it seemed as if the machine could not possibly get through. If we had attempted to turn about, we would surely have been stuck; there was nothing to do but follow the best ruts and go straight on, hoping for better things. The dread of coming to a standstill and being obliged to get out in that eight or ten inches of uninviting mud was a very appreciable factor in our discomfort. Fortunately, the clutch held well and the motor was not stalled. When we passed the corner beyond the cemetery the road was much better, though still so soft the high speed could be used only occasionally.

The tank showed a leak, which for some reason increased so rapidly that a pail of water had to be added about every half-mile. At last a pint of bran poured into the tank closed the leak in five minutes.

On reaching Latham it was apparent that Schenectady could not be made before dark, if at all, so we turned to the right into Troy. We had made the two long sides of a triangle over the worst of roads; whereas, had we run from Albany direct to Troy, we could have followed a good road all the way.

The next morning was the 16th of September, the sun was shining brightly and the wind was fresh; the roads were drying every moment, so we did not hurry our departure.

The express office in Albany was telephoned for a new chain that had been ordered, and in about an hour it was delivered. The machine was driven into a side street in front of a metal roofing factory, the tank taken out and so thoroughly repaired it gave no further trouble. It was noon before the work was finished, for the new chain and a new belt to the pump had to be put on, and many little things done which consumed time.

At two o'clock we left Troy. The road to Schenectady in good weather is quite good, but after the rain it was heavy with half-dried mud and deep with ruts. From Schenectady to Fonda, where we arrived at six-thirty, the roads were very bad; however, forty-five miles in four hours and a half was fairly good travelling under the adverse conditions. If the machine had been equipped with an intermediate gear, an average of twelve or fifteen miles could have been easily made. The going was just a little too heavy for the fast speed and altogether too easy for the low, and yet we were obliged to travel for hours on the low gear.

From New York to Buffalo there is a succession of cities and villages which are, for the most part, very attractive, but good hotels are scarce, and as for wayside inns there are none. With the exception of Albany and one or two other cities the hotels are old, dingy, and dirty. Here and there, as in Geneva, a new hotel is found, but to most of the cities the hotels are a disgrace.

The automobile, however, accustoms one to discomforts, and one gets so tired and hungry at night that the shortcomings of the village hotel are overlooked, or not fully realized until seen the next morning by the frank light of day.

Fonda is the occasion of these remarks upon New York hotels.

It was cloudy and threatening when we left Fonda at half-past seven the next morning, and by ten the rain began to fall so heavily and steadily that the roads, none too dry before, were soon afloat.

It was slow going. At St. Johnsville we stopped to buy heavier rubber coats. It did not seem possible we would get through the day without coming to a stop, but, strange to relate, the machine kept on doggedly all day, on the slow gear nearly every mile, without a break of any kind.

It was bad enough from St. Johnsville to Herkimer, but the worst was then to come.

When we came east from Utica to Herkimer, we followed the road on the north side of the valley, and recalled it as hilly but very dry and good. The Endurance Contest was out of Herkimer, through Frankfort and along the canal on the south side of the valley. It was a question whether to follow the road we knew was pretty good or follow the contest route, which presumably was selected as the better.

A liveryman at Herkimer said, "Take my advice and keep on the north side of the valley; the road is hilly, but sandy and drier; if you go through Frankfort, you will find some pretty fierce going; the road is level but cut up and deep with mud, — keep on the north side."

We should have followed that advice, the more so since it coincided with our own impressions; but at the store where we stopped for gasoline, a man who said he drove an automobile advised the road through Frankfort as the better.

It was in Frankfort that several of the contestants in the endurance run came to grief, — right on the main street of the village. There was no sign of pavement, macadam, or gravel, just deep, dark, rich muck; how deep no one could tell; a road so bad it spoke volumes for the shiftlessness and lack of enterprise prevailing in the village.

A little beyond Frankfort there is about a mile of State road, laid evidently to furnish inhabitants an object lesson, — and laid in vain.

A little farther on the black muck road leads between the canal and towpath high up on the left, and a high board fence protecting the railroad tracks on the right; in other words, the highway was the low ground between two elevations. The rains of the week before and the rains of the last two days had converted the road into a vast ditch. We made our way slowly into it, and then seizing an opening ran up onto the towpath, which was of sticky clay and bad enough, but not quite so discouraging as the road. We felt our way along carefully, for the machine threatened every moment to slide either into the canal on the left or down the bank into the road on the right.

Soon we were obliged to turn back to the road and take our chances on a long steady pull on the slow gear. Again and again it seemed as if the motor would stop; several times it was necessary to throw out the clutch, let the motor race, and then throw in the clutch to get the benefit of both the motor and the momentum of the two-hundred pound fly-wheel; it was a strain on the chain and gears, but they held, and the machine would be carried forward ten or twelve feet by the impetus; in that way the worst spots were passed.

Towards Utica the roads were better, though we nearly came to grief in a low place just outside the city.

It required all Wednesday morning to clean and overhaul the machine. Every crevice was filled with mud, and grit had worked into the chain and every exposed part. There was also some lost motion to be taken up to stop a disagreeable pounding. The strain on the new chain had stretched it so a link had to be taken out.

It was two o'clock before we left Utica. A little beyond the outskirts of the city the road forks, the right is the road to Syracuse, and it is gravelled most of the way. Unfortunately, we took the left fork, and for seven miles ploughed through red clay, so sticky that several times we just escaped being stalled. It was not until we reached Clinton that we discovered our mistake and turned cross country to the right road. The cross-road led through a low boggy meadow that was covered with water, and there we nearly foundered. When the hard gravel of the turnpike was reached, it was with a feeling of irritation that we looked back upon the time wasted in the horrible roads we need not have taken.

The day was bright, and every hour of sun and wind improved the roads, so that by the time we were passing Oneida Castle the going was good. It was dark when we passed through Fayetteville; a little beyond our reserve gallon of gasoline was put in the tank and the run was made over the toll-road to Syracuse on "short rations."

A well-kept toll-road is a boon in bad weather, but to the driver of an automobile the stations are a great nuisance; one is scarcely passed before another is in sight; it is stop, stop, stop. There are so many old toll-roads upon which toll is no longer collected that one is apt to get in the habit of whizzing through the gates so fast that the keepers, if there be any, have no time to come out, much less to collect the rates.

It was cold the next morning when we started from Syracuse, and it waxed colder and colder all day long.

The Endurance Contest followed the direct road to Rochester, going by way of Port Byron, Lyons, Palmyra, and Pittsford. That road is neither interesting nor good. Even if one is going to Rochester, the roads are better to the south; but as we had no intention of visiting the city again, we took Genesee Street and intended to follow it into Buffalo.

The old turnpike leads to the north of Auburn and Seneca Falls, but we turned into the Falls for dinner. In trying to find and follow the turnpike we missed it, and ran so far to the north that we were within seven or eight miles of Rochester, so near, in fact, that at the village of Victor the inhabitants debated whether it would not be better to run into Rochester and thence to Batavia by Bergen rather than southwest through Avon and Caledonia.

Having started out with the intention of passing Rochester, we were just obstinate enough to keep to the south. The result was that for nearly the entire day the machine was laboring over the indifferent roads that usually lie just between two main travelled highways. It was not until dusk that the gravelled turnpike leading into Avon was found, and it was after seven when we drew up in front of the small St. George Hotel.

The glory of Avon has departed. Once it was a great resort, with hotels in size almost equal to those now at Saratoga. The Springs were famous and people came from all parts of the country. The hotels are gone, some burned, some destroyed, but old registers are preserved, and they bear the signatures of Webster, Clay, and many noted men of that generation.

The Springs are a mile or two away; the water is supposed to possess rare medicinal virtues, and invalids still come to test its potency, but there is no life, no gayety; the Springs and the village are quite forlorn.

At the St. George we found good rooms and a most excellent supper. In the office after supper, with chairs tipped back and legs crossed, the older residents told many a tale of the palmy days of Avon when carriages filled the Square and the streets were gay with people in search of pleasure rather than health.

It was a quick run the next morning through Caledonia to Le Roy over roads hard and smooth as a floor.

Just out of Le Roy we met a woman, with a basket of eggs, driving a horse that seemed sobriety itself. We drew off to one side and stopped the machine to let her pass. The horse stopped, and unfortunately she gave a "yank" on one of the reins, turning the horse to one side; then a pull on the other rein, turning the horse sharply to the other side. This was too much for the animal, and he kept on around, overturning the light buckboard and upsetting the woman, eggs, and all into the road. The horse then kicked himself free and trotted off home.

The woman, fortunately, was not injured, but the eggs were, and she mournfully remarked they were not hers, and that she was taking them to market for a neighbor. The wagon was slightly damaged. Relieved to find the woman unhurt, the damage to wagon and eggs was more than made good; we took the woman home in the automobile, — her first ride.

It does not matter how little to blame one may be for a runaway; the fact remains that were it not for the presence of the automobile on the road the particular accident would not have occurred. The fault may be altogether on the side of the inexperienced or careless driver, but none the less the driver of the automobile feels in a certain sense that he has been the immediate cause, and it is impossible to describe the feeling of relief one experiences when it turns out that no one is injured.

A machine could seldom meet a worse combination than a fairly spirited horse, a nervous woman, and a large basket of eggs. With housewifely instincts, the woman was sure to think first of the eggs.

We stopped at Batavia for dinner, and made the run into Buffalo in exactly two hours, arriving at four o'clock.

We ran the machine to the same station, and found unoccupied the same rooms we had left four weeks and two days before. It seemed an age since that Wednesday, August 24, when we started out, so much had transpired, every hour had been so eventful. Measured by the new things we had seen and the strange things that had happened, the interval was months not weeks.

A man need not go beyond his doorstep to find a new world; his own country, however small, is a universe that can never be fully explored. And yet such is the perversity of human nature that we know all countries better than our own; we travel everywhere except at home. The denizens of the earth in their wanderings cross each other en route like letters; all Europe longs to see Niagara, all America to see Mont Blanc, and yet whoever sees the one sees the other, for the grandeur of both is the same. It does not matter whether a vast volume of water is pouring over the sharp edge of a cliff, or a huge pile of scarred and serrated rock rises to the heavens, the grandeur is the same; it is not the outward form we stand breathless before, but the forces of nature which produce every visible and invisible effect. The child of nature worships the god within the mountains and the spirit behind the waters; whereas we in our great haste observe only the outward form, see only the falling waters and the towering peaks.

It is good for every man to come at least once in his life in contact with some overpowering work of nature; it is better for most men to never see but one; let the memory linger, let not the impression be too soon effaced, rather let it sink deep into the heart until it becomes a part of life.

Steam has impaired the imagination. Such is the facility of modern transportation that we ride on the ocean today and sit at the feet of the mountains tomorrow.

Nowadays we see just so much of nature as the camera sees and no more; our vision is but surface deep, our eyes are but two clear, bright lenses with nothing behind, not even a dry plate to record the impressions. It is a physiological fact that the cells of the brain which first receive impressions from the outward organs of sense may be reduced to a condition of comparative inactivity by too rapid succession of sights, sounds, and other sensations. We see so much that we see nothing. To really see is to fully comprehend, therefore our capacity for seeing is limited. No man has really seen Niagara, no man has ever really seen Mont Blanc; for that matter, no man has even fully comprehended so much as a grain of sand; therefore the universe is at one's doorstep.

Nature is a unit; it is not a whole made up of many diverse parts, but is a whole which is inherent in every part. No two persons see the same things in a blossoming flower; to the botanist it is one thing, to the poet another, to the painter another, to the child a bit of bright color, to the maiden an emblem of love, to the heart-broken woman a cluster of memories; to no two is it precisely the same.

The longer we look at anything, however simple, the deeper it penetrates into our being until it becomes a part of us. In time we learn to know the tree that shades our porch, but years elapse before we are on friendly terms, and a lifetime is spent before the gnarled giant admits us to intimate companionship. Trees are filled with reserve; when denuded of their neighbors, they stand in melancholy solitude until the leaves fall for the last time, until their branches wither, and their trunks ring hollow with decay.

And if we never really see or know or understand the nature which is about us, how is it possible that we should ever comprehend the people we meet? What is the use of trying to know an Englishman or a Frenchman when we do not know an American? What is the use of struggling with the obstacle of a foreign tongue, when our own will not suffice for the communication of thoughts? The only light that we have is at home; travellers are men groping in the dark; they fancy they see much, but for the most part they see nothing. No great teacher has ever been a great traveller. Buddha, Confucius, and Mahomet never left the confines of their respective countries. Plato lived in Athens; Shakespeare travelled between London and Stratford; these great souls found it quite sufficient to know themselves and the vast universe as reflected from the eyes of those about them. But then they are the exceptions.

For most men — including geniuses — travel and deliberate observation are good, since most men will not observe at home. Such is the singularity of our nature that we ignore the interesting at home to study the commonplace abroad. We never notice a narrow and crooked street in Boston or lower New York, whereas a narrow and crooked street in London fills us with an ecstasy of delight. We never visit the Metropolitan Art Museum, but we cross Europe to visit galleries of lesser interest. We choose a night boat down the majestic Hudson, and we suffer untold discomforts by day on crowded little boats paddling down the comparatively insignificant Rhine.

Every country possesses its own peculiar advantages and beauties. There is no desert so barren, no mountains so bleak, no woods so wild that to those who dwell therein their home is not beautiful. The Esquimau would not exchange his blinding waste of snow and dark fields of water for the luxuriance of tropic vegetation. Why should we exchange the glories of the land we live in for the footworn and sight-worn, the thumbed and fingered beauties of other lands? If we desire novelty and adventure, seek it in the unexplored regions of the great Northwest; if we crave grandeur, visit the Yellowstone and the fastnesses of the Rockies; if we wish the sublime, gaze in the mighty chasm of the Cañon of the Colorado, where strong men weep as they look down; if we seek desolation, traverse the alkali plains of Arizona where the trails are marked by bones of men and beasts; but if the heart yearns for beauty more serene, go forth among the habitations of men where fields are green and sheltering woods offer refuge from the noonday sun, where rivers ripple with laughter, and the great lakes smile in soft content.

Unhappy the man who does not believe his country the best on earth and his people the chosen of men.

The promise of automobiling is knowledge of one's own land. The confines of a city are stifling to the sport; the machine snorts with impatience on dusty pavements filled with traffic, and seeks the freedom of country roads. Within a short time every hill and valley within a radius of a hundred miles is a familiar spot; the very houses become known, and farmers shout friendly greetings as the machine flies by, or lend helping hands when it is in distress.

Within a season or two it will be an everyday sight to see people journeying leisurely from city to city; abandoned taverns will be reopened, new ones built, and the highways, long since deserted by pleasure, will once more be gay with life.

CHAPTER 18

Through Canada Home

HOME

We left Buffalo, Saturday the 20th, at four o'clock for St. Catharines. At the Bridge we were delayed a short time by customs formalities.

In going out of the States it is necessary to enter the machine for export and return, otherwise on coming in again the officials on our side will collect duty on its full value.

On crossing to the Canadian side, it is necessary to enter the machine and pay the duty of thirty per cent on its valuation. The machine is entered for temporary use in Canada, under a law providing for the use of bicycles, hunting and fishing outfits, and sporting implements generally, and the port at which you intend to go out is named; a receipt for the duty deposited is given and the money is either refunded at the port of exit or the machine is simply identified by the officials, and remittance made upon returning the receipt to the port of entry.

It is something of a bother to deposit thirty per cent upon the valuation of an automobile, but the Canadian officials are obliging; and where it is clearly apparent that there is no intention of selling the machine in the province, they are not exacting as to the valuation; a two-thousand-dollar machine may be valued pretty low as second-hand. If, however, anything should occur which would make it desirable to leave or sell the machine in Canada, a re-entry at full market valuation should be made immediately, otherwise the machine is — very properly — subject to confiscation.

Parties running across the river from Buffalo for a day's run are not bothered at all. The officials on both sides let the machines pass, but anyone crossing Canada would better comply with all regulations and save trouble.

It was six o'clock when we arrived at St. Catharines. The Wendell Hotel happens to be a mineral water resort with baths for invalids, and therefore much better as a hotel than most Canadian houses; in fact, it may be said once for all, that Canadian hotels, with the exception of two or three, are very poor; they are as indifferent in the cities as in the smaller towns, being for the most part dingy and dirty. But what Canada lacks in hotels she more than makes up in roads. Miles upon miles of well-made and well-kept gravel roads cross the province of Ontario in every direction. The people seem to appreciate the economy of good hard highways over which teams can draw big loads without undue fatigue.

We left St. Catharines at nine o'clock Sunday morning, taking the old Dundas road; this was a mistake, the direct road to Hamilton being the better. Off the main travelled roads we found a good deal of sand; but that was our fault, for it was needless to take these little travelled by-ways. Again, out of Hamilton to London we did not follow the direct and better road; this was due to error in directions given us at the drugstore where we stopped for gasoline.

Gasoline is not so easily obtained in Canada as in the States; it is not to be had at all in many of the small villages, and in the cities it is not generally kept in any quantity. One drugstore in Hamilton had half-a-dozen six-ounce bottles neatly put up and labelled "Gasoline: Handle with Care;" another had two gallons, which we purchased. The price was high, but the price of gasoline is the very least of the concerns of automobiling.

On the way to London a forward spring collapsed entirely. Binding the broken leaves together with wire we managed to get in all right, but the next morning we were delayed an hour while a wheelwright made a more permanent repair.

Monday, the 22d, was one of the record days. Leaving London at half-past nine we took the Old Sarnia Gravel for Sarnia, some seventy miles away. With scarcely a pause, we flew over the superb road, hard gravel every inch of it, and into Sarnia at one o'clock for luncheon.

Over an hour was spent in lunching, ferrying across the river, and getting through the two custom-houses.

Canada is an anachronism. Within the lifetime of men now living, the Dominion will become a part of the United States; this is fate not politics, evolution not revolution, destiny not design. How it will come about no man can tell; that it will come about is as certain as fate.

With an area almost exactly that of the United States, Canada has a population of but five millions, or about one-fifteenth the population of this country. Between 1891 and 1901 the population of the Dominion increased only five hundred thousand, or about ten per cent, as against an increase of fourteen millions, or twenty-one per cent, in this country.

For a new country in a new world Canada stagnates. In the decade referred to Chicago alone gained more in population than the entire Dominion. The fertile province of Ontario gained but fifty-four thousand in the ten years, while the States of Michigan, Indiana, and Ohio, which are near by, gained each nearly ten times as much; and the gain of New York, lying just across the St. Lawrence, was over twelve hundred thousand. The total area of these four States is about four-fifths that of Ontario, and yet their increase of population in ten years more than equals the entire population of the province.

In population, wealth, industries, and resources Ontario is the Dominion's gem; yet in a decade she could attract and hold but fifty-odd thousand persons, — not quite all the children born within her borders.

All political divisions aside, there is no reason in the world why population should be dense on the west bank of the Detroit River and sparse on the east; why people should teem to suffocation to the south of the St. Lawrence and not to the north.

These conditions are not normal, and sooner or later must change. It is not in the nature of things that this North American continent should be arbitrarily divided in its most fertile midst by political lines, and by and by it will be impossible to keep the multiplying millions south of the imaginary line from surging across into the rich vacant territory to the north. The outcome is inevitable; neither diplomacy nor statecraft can prevent it.

When the population of this country is a hundred or a hundred and fifty millions the line will have disappeared. There may be a struggle of some kind over some real or fancied grievance, but, struggle or no struggle, it is not for man to oppose for long inevitable tendencies. In the long run, population, like water, seeks its level; in adjacent territories, the natural advantages and attractions of which are alike, the population tends strongly to become equally dense; political conditions and differences in race and language may for a time hold this tendency in check, but where race and language are the same, political barriers must soon give way.

All that has preserved Canada from absorption up to this time is the existence of those mighty natural barriers, the St. Lawrence and the great lakes. As population increases in the Northwest, where the dividing line is known only to surveyors, the situation will become critical. Already the rush to the Klondike has produced trouble in Alaska. The aggressive miners from this side, who constitute almost the entire population, submit with ill-grace to Canadian authority. They do not like it, and Dawson or some near point may yet become a second Johannesburg.

In all controversies so far, Canada has been as belligerent as England has been conciliatory. With rare tact and diplomacy England has avoided all serious differences with this country over Canadian matters without at the same time offending the pride of the Dominion; just how long this can be kept up no man can tell; but not for more than a generation to come, if so long.

So far as the people of Canada are concerned, practically all would be opposed to any form of annexation. The great majority of the people are Englishmen at heart and very English in thought, habit, speech, and accent; they are much more closely allied to the mother country than to this; and they are exceedingly patriotic.

They do not like us because they rather fear us, — not physically, not as man against man, — but fear our overwhelming size and increasing importance, fear for the future, fear what down deep in their hearts many of them know must come. Their own increasing independence has taught them the sentimental and unsubstantial character of the ties binding them to England, and yet they know full well that with those ties severed their independence would soon disappear.

Michigan roads are all bad, but some are worse than others.

About Port Huron is sand. Out of the city there is a rough stone road made of coarse limestone; it did not lead in the direction we wished to go, but by taking it we were able to get away from the river and the lake and into a country somewhat less sandy.

Towards evening, while trying to follow the most direct road into Lapeer, and which an old lady said was good "excepting one hill, which isn't very steep," we came to a hill which was not steep, but sand, deep, bottomless, yellow sand. Again and again the machine tried to scale that hill; it was impossible. There was nothing to do but turn about and find a better road.

An old farmer, who had been leaning on the fence watching our efforts, sagely remarked:

"I was afeard your nag would balk on that thar hill; it is little the worst rise anywhere's about here, and most of us know better'n to attempt it; but I guess you're a stranger."

We dined at Lapeer, and by dark made the run of eighteen miles into

Flint, where we arrived at eight-thirty. We had covered one hundred and forty miles in twelve hours, including all stops, delays, and difficulties.

It was the Old Sarnia Gravel which helped us on our journey that day.

At Flint another new chain was put on, and also a rear sprocket with new differential gears. The old sprocket was badly worn and the teeth of the gears showed traces of hard usage. A new spring was substituted for the broken, and the machine was ready for the last lap of the long run.

Leaving Flint on Friday morning, the 26th, a round-about run was made to Albion for the night. The intention was to follow the line of the Grand Trunk through Lansing, Battle Creek, and Owosso, but, over-persuaded by some wiseacres, a turn was made to Jackson, striking there the old State road.

The roads through Lansing and Battle Creek can be no worse than the sandy and hilly turnpike. Now and then a piece of gravel is found, but only for a short distance, ending usually in sand.

On Saturday the run was made from Albion to South Bend. As far as Kalamazoo and for some distance beyond the roads were hilly and for the most part sandy, — a disgrace to so rich and prosperous a State.

Through Paw Paw and Dowagiac some good stretches of gravel were found and good time was made. It was dark when we reached the Oliver House in South Bend, a remarkably fine hotel for a place of the size.

The run into Chicago next day was marked by no incident worthy of note. As already stated, the roads of Indiana are generally good, and fifteen miles an hour can be averaged with ease.

It was four o'clock, Sunday, September 28, when the machine pulled into the stable whence it departed nearly two months before. The electricity was turned off, with a few expiring gasps the motor stopped.

Taking into consideration the portions of the route covered twice, the side trips, and making some allowance for lost roads, the distance covered was over twenty-six hundred miles; a journey, the hardships and annoyances of which were more, far more, than counterbalanced by the delights.

No one who has not travelled through America on foot, horseback, or awheel knows anything about the variety and charm of this great country. We traversed but a small section, and yet it seemed as if we had spent weeks and months in a strange land. The sensations from day to day are indescribable. It is not alone the novel sport, but the country and the people along the way seemed so strange, possibly because automobiling has its own point of view, and certainly people have their own and widely varying views of automobiling. In the presence of the machine people everywhere become for the time-being childlike and naive, curious and enthusiastic; they lose the veneer of sophistication, and are as approachable and companionable as children. Automobiling is therefore doubly delightful in these early days of the sport. By and by, when the people become accustomed to the machine, they will resume their habit of indifference, and we shall see as little of them as if we were riding or driving.

With some exceptions everyone we met treated the machine with a consideration it did not deserve. Even those who were put to no little inconvenience with their horses seldom showed the resentment which might have been expected under the circumstances. On the contrary, they seemed to recognize the right of the strange car to the joint use of the highway, and to blame their horses for not behaving better. Verily, forbearance is an American virtue.

The machine itself stood the journey well, all things considered. It lacked power and was too light for such a severe and prolonged test; but, when taken apart to be restored to perfect condition, it was astonishing how few parts showed wear. The bearings had to be adjusted and one or two new ones put in. A number of little things were done, but the mechanic spent only forty hours' time all told in making the machine quite as good as new. A coat of paint and varnish removed all outward signs of rough usage.

However, one must not infer that automobiling is an inexpensive way of touring, but measured by the pleasure derived, the expense is as nothing; at the same time look out for the man who says "My machine has not cost me a cent for repairs in six months."

It is singular how reticent owners of automobiles are concerning the shortcomings and eccentricities of their machines; they seem leagued together to deceive one another and the public. The literal truth can be found only in letters of complaint written to the manufacturers. The man who one moment says his machine is a paragon of perfection, sits down the next and writes the factory a letter which would be debarred the mails if left unsealed. Open confession is good for the soul, and owners of automobiles must cultivate frankness of speech, for deep in our innermost hearts we all know that a machine would have so tried the patience of Job that even Bildad the Shuhite would have been silenced.

In the year 1735 a worthy Puritan divine, pastor over a little flock in the town of Malden, made the following entries in his diary:

"*January 31.* — Bought a shay for £27 10s. The Lord grant it may be a comfort and a blessing to my family.

"*March, 1735.* — Had a safe and comfortable journey to York.

"*April 24.* — Shay overturned, with my wife and I in it; yet neither of us much hurt. Blessed be our generous Preserver! Part of the shay, as it lay upon one side, went over my wife, and yet she was scarcely anything hurt. How wonderful the preservation.

"*May 5.* — Went to the Beach with three of the children. The beast being frighted, when we were all out of the shay, overturned and broke it. I desire it (I hope I desire it) that the Lord would teach me suitably to repent this Providence, and make suitable remarks on it, and to be suitably affected with it. Have I done well to get me a shay? Have I not been proud or too fond of this convenience? Do I exercise the faith in the divine care and protection which I ought to do? Should I not be more in my study and less fond of diversion? Do I not withhold more than is meet from pious and charitable uses?

"*May 15.* — Shay brought home; mending cost thirty shillings. Favored in this beyond expectation.

"*May 16.* — My wife and I rode to Rumney Marsh. The beast frighted several times.

"*June 4.* — Disposed of my shay to Rev. Mr. White."

Moral. — Under conditions of like adversity, let every chauffeur cultivate the same spirit of humility, — and look for a Deacon White.

THE END.

Index

Webster, Daniel, 115
Wellesley, 104
West Otis, 98
West Wrentham, 152
Western New York, 56, 59
Whipple, 140
White, Deacon, 188
Whitman, Walt, 129
Wickliff, 30
Willoughby, 30
wine, 33, 111, 145–147
Winthrop, Governor, 110
Woburn Street, 115
women, 10, 34, 83–85, 90, 93, 106,
   129–131, 142, 155, 156, 169

Worcester, 98–101, 103, 104, 143,
   156
Worcester Street, 104
Worcester Turnpike, 104
Wyoming Valleys, 70

yachting, 20
Yonkers, 172
Young Americans, 165
Young Sicilian, 148, 149
Young, Brigham, 84
Yquem of '48, 147

Zion Temple, 13

www.ingramcontent.com/pod-product-compliance
Lightning Source LLC
Chambersburg PA
CBHW021053090426
42738CB00006B/313